Winsome Womanhood

"Shelley Noonan has done it again! This Nebraska farm wife who helped bring us *The Companion Guide to Beautiful Girlhood* has applied her godly wisdom to yet another classic masterpiece of Christian literature. Here, she not only revises Margaret Sangster's original 1900 publication but adds questions, Bible studies, and activities to turn this lovely book into an in-depth study in womanhood for ladies aged 15–20 and their mothers.

"This book gives many principles from God's Word and is not without a large dose of the spirit and heart of its author. Those who know Shelley will see in this book much of her godly life and winsome personality. Those who do not know her may rest assured that she truly partakes of the winsome womanhood of which this book speaks. I highly recommend this book and will include it in future editions of *Far Above Rubies.*

Lynda Coats
Author of Far Above Rubies and Blessed in the Man

"Books from the past are often treasure chests full of beautiful gems from days gone by, and Shelley has found just that in *Winsome Womanhood.*

"She has polished and shined it with loving care for new generations of young Christian girls who desperately need the mentoring that is found within its pages. What a joy it will be for mothers and daughters to rediscover together the wisdom today's girls need to grow from Christian girlhood to Christian womanhood."

Kathy Kin
Homeschool Mom and Education Consultant
Owner of My Family Bookshelf

WINSOME WOMANHOOD
~Daybreak~

Familiar talks on life
and conduct by
Margaret Elizabeth Sangster

Revised and expanded by
SHELLEY NOONAN

Pumpkin Seed
P R E S S

Winsome Womanhood ~ Daybreak

Copyright © 2001, Shelley Noonan

*Revised and expanded from the original edition of Winsome Womanhood
written by Margaret E. Sangster, Copyright 1900 by Fleming H. Revell
Company. Chapter 6 & 7 of this book was revised and expanded from
another book by Margaret Sangster, Copyright 1897 titled Life On High
Levels ~ Familiar Talks.*

All Scripture quotations unless otherwise marked are taken from the New
King James Version. Copyright © 1979, 1980, 1982. Thomas Nelson Inc.,
Publishers. Scripture quotations marked KJV are from *The Holy Bible, King
James Version.* Copyright © 1977, 1984, Thomas Nelson Inc., Publishers.

ISBN: 0-9700273-3-8

For more information or
to order additional copies, please contact:

Pumpkin Seed Press, 43668 355th Ave., Humphrey, Nebraska, 68642
(402) 923-1682

Pumpkin Seed
P R E S S

winsome \ WIN-sum \ *adjective:*

1. Cheerful; merry; gay; light-hearted.
2. Causing joy or pleasure; gladsome; pleasant.

Webster's Revised Unabridged Dictionary, © 1996, 1998 MICRA, Inc.

Table of Contents

Preface

A HUNDRED YEARS AGO, THIS BOOK WAS WRITTEN by a remarkable woman with a clear vision for Christian womanhood. One hundred years later, life is quite different but the inherent truths of this book remain the same. Truth is timeless. We, as mothers, have lost the focus of teaching our daughters what it means to be women. We have been brought up to believe that one way or another it will just happen. Lead a good life and your daughter will learn by osmosis. Sadly, this does not happen in most instances. I believe now is the time to harken back to the day when values were taught with intent, a time when mothers mentored daughters, an era when timeless truths were passed from generation to generation. Young women were purposefully taught what it meant to be women in the world in which they lived. By exercising the gentle art of mothering, you too can teach your daughters what it means to be women in their world.

The original book, written by Margaret Elizabeth Sangster in 1900 and entitled *Winsome Womanhood*, was divided into four parts: "Daybreak," for girls fifteen to twenty; "High Noon" for women twenty-one to fifty; "Eventide" for women fifty to sixty-five; "The Rounded Life" for women sixty-five and up. This revision and study guide will cover only the first part of this four-part book. "Daybreak" is intended to be used by mothers and their daughters of fifteen to twenty years of age.

The revisions to this fine book were intended to make the way easier for the modern reader. Although truth is truth, some gentle editing was applied to improve the flow of ideas and limit digressions. Chapters Six and Seven were added from another book that Mrs. Sangster wrote called *Life on High* (Levels copyright 1897).

It is my hope and prayer that this book will be a tool of mentorship and molding for mothers to use in relationship with their daughters. I pray its enjoyment will be a growth time treasured by both mother and daughter. Finally, I echo the desire Margaret expressed: "...that all who read these pages accept the Lord Christ as their Master and Friend."

Shelley Noonan
October 2000

Foreword

THIS LITTLE BOOK HAS BEEN WRITTEN for women, with
a wish and hope that it may prove suggestive and helpful to the girl in her teens, who faces so many problems,
and stands before an unknown future. God is so good to us all in
these days of large movement and increasing privilege, that more
than ever before we owe to Him a debt of grateful love.

Our whole-hearted devotion is not too much to offer Him. It
is our highest honor that we may work for God in this world of
His, and that every day may be a stepping stone toward Heaven.

I have called this book *Winsome Womanhood* because it is
my firm belief that we are strongest as we are gentlest, that the
"loving are the daring" and that the ideal Christian woman
should be especially serene, tender and full of charm. In the
twenty-first century, with Martha, she may be enterprising, busy
and efficient, but with Mary also, she shall find time to sit at the
Master's feet.

Never has there been greater occasion for the Christian
woman to take a firm stand for the principles which she has

avowed. Never in our modern days has society so insidiously opposed the claims of simple Christianity. The opportunity not only invites; it is urgent and imperative and woman cannot evade it. May all who read these pages accept the Lord Christ as their Master and Friend.

Margaret Elizabeth Sangster
1900

❧ *Biographical Note*

SANGSTER, MARGARET ELIZABETH MUNSON
BORN: FEBRUARY 22, 1838, NEW ROCHELLE, NY, USA
DIED: JUNE 3, 1912, SOUTH ORANGE, NJ, USA

Margaret Elizabeth Munson Sangster was, from an early age, a voracious reader. Writing became a natural event for her because of this early passion. Her first published story, "Little Janey" (1855), won her a appointment to write 100 children's stories. She married George Sangster in 1858, paused in her writing career and starting again in 1871, after his death.

She wrote for periodicals, became an assistant editor of a magazine and editor of *Harper's Bazaar*. Throughout her career, Margaret continued to write articles, essays and letters reflecting her belief that she had a "mission to girlhood" to be a Christian leader to young women. She wrote numerous books, including, *An Autobiography: From My Youth Up; Personal Reminiscences* (1909). Her writings were enjoyed for their pious, cheerful and sentimental flavor. The practical application—common sense and godly wisdom—make her books timeless.

How to Use
Winsome Womanhood ~ Daybreak

GENERAL GUIDANCE

Winsome Womanhood ~ Daybreak was intended to help mothers to mentor daughters between the ages of fifteen and twenty years. The book begins with the chapter, "The Girl of Fifteen," and spans a total of seven areas of the young woman's life, ending with "Her Occupation."

The general plan is to read one chapter of *Winsome Womanhood ~ Daybreak* every week, choosing a time that works for both of you. The chapter could be read out loud together or individually. The Mother/Daughter questions are to be done individually, writing the answers in personal journals. Then, at the time you decide to meet, discuss the questions each of you feel are important and read your journal entries. The Bible studies are done throughout the week individually, to be shared (if you desire) when you meet. This provides seven weeks of curriculum for you and your daughter (Prov. 14:22b).

1. Look at your calendar and choose seven weeks to undertake this study. Establish a day and time to begin. By choosing a set

time, your goal is clearly marked and easier to reach (Hab. 2:2).

2. Begin with prayer. Discuss what both of your goals are. Do you want a closer relationship? Do you wish to create a life-long memory? Do you, daughter, want your mother to teach you certain things? Ask God to guide you each time you meet (Ps. 25:4-5).

3. Expect God to do great things in your relationship (Eph. 3:20)!

COMPANION PORTIONS

Five sections have been added to the end of each chapter of *Winsome Womanhood ~ Daybreak*, as follows:

Mother to Mother

The "Mother to Mother" segment of the book is meant to give mothers a vision for what they can accomplish in a chapter. The memories and ideas can be used as encouragement and to elaborate on the goals to be reached during that week.

Journal Questions

"…we spend our years as a tale that is told" (Ps. 90:9). The intent of this section was to have mother and daughter choose one or several of the questions and record their thoughts about it in a journal. One question could be pondered and journalled every day or choose the one(s) you have the strongest feelings about. A journal can be a window into your soul, a way to record your innermost feelings. Take a quiet, unhurried moment to record your reactions on the crisp, smooth pages of your journal. To take it a step further, record the happenings of your day or a memory that has buoyed to the surface. Chronicle what truth God has taught you through His Word, how He has undertaken for you, or how prayer was answered.

Bible Study

The best way we can discover the purpose for our lives, and gain insight on how to live lives pleasing to God, is to read His Word. The Bible study section will be designed to teach you how to develop and maintain a relationship with God. If you don't understand something, cry out to God for He promises in Jeremiah 33:3, *"Call to Me, and I will answer you, and show you great and mighty things, which you do not know."*

I encourage you to study the Bible by looking up and reading each verse. A Bible dictionary will help if there are words or phrases you do not understand. A Bible concordance will also be of assistance, providing all verses associated with a given word. At times, when you sense there might be more to a particular Scripture, you can read what another person gleaned from the passage in a Bible commentary. In order to create a permanent record of your discoveries, read Chapter Two, Project Five for suggestions.

Projects

Enriching exercises to enhance your experience are suggested in this portion. They were added so mother and daughter can participate in fun activities together, explore different opportunities, develop talents and learn skills that will benefit the whole family.

Resources

This portion of the book contains a list of sources from which you can gain more information about a particular subject. There are also run offs for your personal quiet time, prayer time, goal setting, chore chart and recipes.

The Girl of Fifteen

❧ One

"WHERE THE BROOK AND RIVER MEET"

IT MAKES NO LITTLE DIFFERENCE TO THE GIRL of fifteen whether or not she is the oldest daughter of her parents, or occupies the position of middle child, where she touches hands with the young people who are grown up and with the little ones below her, or again, is the baby of the group. In the last position, that of the youngest daughter in a household of several children, she is considered and treated as a mere child when she is fifteen. But if she were the oldest, many duties would fall to her lot, and she would be regarded as almost a woman. Being the middle daughter has certain advantages, and certain handicaps, which neither the oldest or the youngest girl in the family may possess or disclaim. Unless her family is very well-to-do, she may have to wear "hand-me-downs" while her older sisters are taking college courses. She is the one who helps her mother at odd seasons with the housekeeping, mends her father's clothes, plays football and tennis with her brothers and takes care of the little ones. She is fifteen and, as the middle girl, a sort of clasp of the family. The eldest daughter and second oldest have had their share of intimacy with their mother.

A young woman of fifteen has a peculiar and individual question to settle. What she is now forecasts what she may be, indeed what she will be twenty years hence, when life with its broad opportunities and obligations has made her its own. She now stands where the little limpid brook, with its narrow silvery thread and flower-bordered banks, meets the brimming full-bosomed river, and it's impossible not to love her, not to be wistful for her, not to pray for her, if one has in her own heart the memory of the sweet days she lived when she herself was fifteen and a daughter of some happy home.

Winsome and clever, or thoughtful and brooding, merry or quiet, according to her temperament, the girl of fifteen is in some ways a riddle to her mother, and in many ways a puzzle to herself. She is no longer a child to play freely with her mates in the games which delighted her at ten. She is not yet a woman, even though she may have womanly tastes and aspirations. On some subjects, for instance her dress, her amusements, her studies, she has very decided views. She is daily gaining in breadth and independence. At the same time, she is still under her mother's wing and accustomed to refer all questions at issue to her for settlement as the final authority. At this time she needs more than ever the mother's loving guardianship, and the wise mother keeps her daughter very close to her side in confidential affection, in daily life, in the purest and most intimate association. For the little woman is passing through a transformation. Nowhere else can she be safe and as sheltered as in the sweet seclusion of the home. If the daughter is sent away to school, the choice should be a matter of careful thought and personal investigation into the status of the school. The atmosphere of the institution, the character of the teachers and students would need to measure up to the family's standards. At fifteen a young girl is full of enthusiasm. She adores her favorite teacher; she worships the classmate who seems to her to be beautiful and faultless; she makes many sacrifices for her friends, and chameleon-like, unless she is of strong character, she takes on the color, absorbs the manner and reflects the opinion of her companions. If she desires the finest intellectual discipline available today, she may be prepared for college at home or in a good preparatory school. During this time, lessons in practical housewifery should also be taught and learned with diligence. The best school of domestic arts is in the mother's own kitchen and house. A college graduate, however profound and brilliant, however fully furnished mentally, is hardly fitted to be an all-around woman unless she practically understands cooking and general home management. At this age, while being taught as she was being raised, a girl can take over and practice fully the domestic arts.

The reserves of girlhood are an unfathomed sea. For no reason she can explain, the young girl often withholds her thoughts and fancies from her parents and folds herself in secrecy, like a rosebud not yet ready to bloom. It may be that her mother, who is her natural confidante, has been so busy and so cumbered with outside service, that she has lost her child's heart. When this occurs it is a deplorable misfortune. For a daughter's first refuge should be her mother, her next best shield, her father. Now and then it happens that a much-occupied father has a special understanding of his little girl, not grasped by her mother. Her inexperience needs a guide, and she must be piloted over and across the perils which lie between her and the happy days awaiting her farther on.

All who are associated with a girl of fifteen have observed her fondness of clothing, sweets, and her indifference to overshoes and thick boots. Hers is the bread-and-butter age, when she scorns precautions and is averse to the whole machinery of prudence. With a fatal facility she picks up and adopts the college slang from her brothers or the catch-all slang from the street. She needs frequent reminders of her duty to her mother tongue even when she is in the home.

It is well for our young girl if she forms the habit of going every day by herself for a little quiet time of reading her Bible and praying in the morning and at night. When she was a little girl she was taught to say her prayers. Now she must enter the court of the Most High and, for her own soul's sake, confess her sins, ask grace to resist temptation and commune with her heavenly Father. No earthly love, no tenderness of parent or wisdom of preceptor, can impart to her at this time the strength, the grace and the beauty which will be hers, as she seeks the throne of our ever blessed Immanuel and turns to Him as Master and Friend. At fifteen she may well begin, if she has not already done this. This is a good time to begin to establish this relationship with Christ in the privacy of her quiet time. A room of her very own should be every young girl's retreat. Here she may enjoy the half-hours for devotion which tend to the soul's growth and may read and study and entertain her girlfriends. In this her den, her bower, her nook, her special fancies may be indulged and her individuality find fit expression.

If a girl admit me to her room, I need no other interpreter of her character. Her daintiness, her delicacy, her fondness for art, her little fads and caprices are here revealed. Does she care for athletics? Her room tells the story. Her guitar and flute, her books on her bedside table, her closet explain her, for wherever we live we set our seal, and this unconsciously. The untidy girl keeps her room in chaos and confusion: it looks as if swept by a small tornado. The orderly girl has a place for each belonging and puts it there without effort and without fuss. As for the room itself, it may be plain to bareness, or beautifully luxurious; a cell or a shrine, it owes its grace or lack of charm more to its occupant than to its paper and paint, its bed and dresser, its rug and chairs. A girl's room is as much an expression of herself as her mother's house is an expression of herself. We need not resign our right to beautiful surroundings because we must keep a strict rein upon expenditure and have an eye to ways and means. Unless a young woman learns early to make the most of her little in hand, she will never be successful when she has a large sum in her stewardship.

At fifteen summers, the young woman should have some money of her own, whether she earns it from a part time job, babysitting, or an allowance from tasks done around the home. Now is the time for her to learn about how to handle the money she has and what to do when she does not have enough to purchase something she desires. Her purse should have sufficient amount to buy her own wardrobes and to cover expenses when going here and there. She should not be in debt, she should have some margin; she should learn judicious saving, as well as careful spending and, at fifteen, it should be her custom to lay aside a portion of her means for the Lord's treasury.

One final word. A sensitive girl often suffers from the teasing jabs of her brothers and from the thoughtless despotism of her older sisters. She has her rights and privileges, and among them is immunity from needless jesting and careless tyranny. Nor ought a young girl be reproved in public nor held up to ridicule in front of others. Expect from her the performance of her regular daily duties, in the task-work of school, and the routine of the home, but include her in the simple household pleasures. Above all, surround her with the protection of considerate politeness. If she is brusque and short with you, be the more civil to her. If she is willful, treat her with gentleness. If she is disturbed and disquieted, find out the reason. Be true to her, and expect from her the truth. Teach her now how to honor and care for her body and how to conserve her health. And above all things, love her. Let her know and feel that she is treasured for who she is. And let this be her secret of strength: that she is not her own, but bought with a price, even the precious blood of Christ. So she may sing for Him, or work for Him, or live for Him, because her life is His, and He abides in her soul, as in a temple. A friend said of Frances Ridley Havergal, at this beautiful dawning of her life, "Her form was graceful as a flower-stem; her face as bright as the flower itself. She flashed into the room, caroling like a bird. Flashed! …like a burst of sunshine, like a hillside breeze. There was joy in her face, joy in her words, joy in her ways."

Enjoy your girl of fifteen. She makes the world a blither place, where the brook and the river meet.

❧ *Mother to Mother*

"ABOVE ALL ELSE, LOVE HER AND LET HER FEEL HERSELF
BELOVED."

I hate to clean out cabinets. I think this is because I am hopelessly sentimental. I like clean and tidy cupboards but I hate to part with the "memories." Cleaning out the bathroom cabinet used to be my daughter's chore… until she went to college this fall. I think her departure really sunk in on the day I went to clean the bathroom cabinet. It was when I saw her ribbons lined up that I realized she was gone, never again to live in my home as a permanent resident. The blue bow, the white fluffy one, the

Kelly-green polka dot bow... Why didn't she take them with her when she moved into her apartment? As I began to sort through the ribbons, I started searching my mind for the last time I remember her wearing them. Random snapshots, snippets of memories flash before my mind's eye of her scurrying around the house, getting ready for church, her long brown braid hanging down her back with the big white ribbon dangling on the end. That was when she was fourteen. Now she is seventeen and hair that once hung down her back has been cut to a more mature and sophisticated bob.

Where did the time go? The little girl who wore ribbons, bows and braids is only transient, like a butterfly that stays but a summer, like the little bird that rests on your sill before migrating south. Mothers, make the most of the time you have with your daughters. You can share moments that create lifelong memories. The moments you spend teaching and mentoring your daughter will become "forever moments." Don't let this time in life pass without experiencing it with her. Take time this week to savor this season when your daughter is fifteen.

❧ *Mother's Questions*

"WHERE THE BROOK AND RIVER MEET"

1. Take some time to think about the relationship you have with your daughters, particularly the daughter with whom you are doing this study. Whether we want to or not, we treat our children differently because of their different personalities and temperaments. If you were asked to evaluate how you treat each daughter, would it be the same for all? Fair? Different? Can you

explain why this is so and perhaps name some reasons for your behavior. (Mother, share this response with your daughter at your discretion. It is primarily for personal reflection.)

2. Reflect on the daughter(s) you are mentoring through the study of *Winsome Womanhood~ Daybreak*. Describe why you see your daughter as "the little limpid brook with its narrow silvery thread and flower-bordered banks meet(ing) the brimming full-bosomed river" in your journal.

3. What are your dreams for your daughter? What are your dreams for yourself? As you write them in your journal, consider the similarities and differences between them.

4. What are some of your prayers for her? After they are recorded in your journal, you can give thanks as the answers are revealed and document them to show your daughter in later years.

5. Write down some of your own sweet memories from when you were fifteen. Perhaps you wish things had gone differently. How was God at work in your life at that time? Does your past hold lessons for you and your daughter?

6. It is at this time that your daughter needs, more than ever, your loving guardianship. How is it possible to give this to her with out smothering her? Is this difficult for you to do? Why? Try to list some ways you could mother without smothering.

7. Does your daughter have a personal relationship with Jesus Christ? Do you? Find out for sure. In the Bible study for this chapter, the plan that God has laid out for us to become his children is reviewed. Please examine your life, and then prayerfully cover this material with your daughter.

8. Relate to your daughter how and when you came to know Christ. Ask her to tell you her testimony. Encourage her to write it out. Mothers, I want to also encourage you to record your testimony in your journal.

❧ *Daughter's Questions*

"Sometimes I would almost rather have people take
away years of my life than take away moments."

Pearl Bailey (1918–1990)

1. The author used this quote to describe where you are
right now. At fifteen, you are "the little limpid brook with its
narrow silvery thread and flower-bordered banks meet(ing) the
brimming full-bosomed river." How is this like you? How is this
not like you? Enter your thoughts in your journal.

2. In your family, you may be an only child or one of several children. What is your position in the family? How does this
make you special? What makes it hard?

3. Mabel Hale wrote, in *Beautiful Girlhood*, "Why do girls
dream? Because all life is before them, and they cannot help but
anticipate the future that awaits them." What are some of your
dreams for your future? Outline them in your journal. What do
they say about the goals and priorities you have for your life?

4. Prayer is the way we communicate with God. What are
some of your prayers at this time? List them in your journal.

5. What an amazing time of life this is for you! Document
in your journal a particularly happy incident since you have
become fifteen years old. Describe it in vivid detail.

6. According to the author, it is at this time in your life that
you need your mother's loving guardianship more than ever.
Do you believe this is true? Why or why not? Could you list
some ways that your mother could "mother" you without
smothering you?

7. Do you have a personal relationship with Jesus Christ?
God made a plan for you to become His child through His Son,

Jesus Christ. In the Bible study, you and your mother will review
God's plan to make you a part of His family.

8. If you have already accepted Christ as your personal Savior, give your mother the testimony of how this happened.
Describe the event in your journal. Ask your mother to share
when this happened in her life.

❧ *Bible Study*

"THANKS BE TO GOD FOR HIS INDESCRIBABLE GIFT!"

2 Corinthians 9:15

You will always be your mother's daughter, but I need to ask
you a question. Are you a daughter of the King? The following
Bible study will help you determine if you have personally
received Christ as your Savior. Read the following verses and
answer the following questions.

1. 1 John 1:8 - Is there anyone without sin?

2. Romans 3:12 and 23 - According to these passages are
your works good? Are you good enough to enter Heaven?

3. Romans 5:8 - How did God demonstrate His love for
you? For whom did Christ die?

4. 2 Corinthians 5:21 - What was Christ made for you? Why?

5. Romans 6:23 - According to this passage what do you
deserve? Through Christ what do you receive?

6. Romans 10:9 and 10 - What must you do to be saved?
Explain your answer in your own words. According to the Bible,
what four steps must you take? First, look up the meanings of
the following four words in a dictionary and record them. Then
look up the following verses:

Repent ~ Luke 13:3, Mark 1:15
Confess ~ John 1:9, Romans 10:9
Believe ~ Acts 16:31, 1 Timothy 1:16, Hebrews 11:6
Decide ~ 2 Corinthians 6:2, Joshua 24:15

Have you personally received Christ as your Savior? *"I tell you, now is the time of God's favor, now is the day of salvation"* (2 Cor. 6:2). You have an opportunity to become God's child, a daughter of the King! If this is your desire, pour out your heart to the Lord and tell Him what His Scripture has pointed out to you. The Lord loves to hear your voice!

If you have never before confessed your sin, repented and asked Jesus Christ to save you, know that *"The angels are rejoicing"* (Luke 15:10). Take time to tell your mother and write this date and what happened in your journal! Welcome to the family!

❧ *Projects*

"MEN JUDGE US BY THE SUCCESS OF OUR EFFORTS. GOD LOOKS AT THE EFFORTS THEMSELVES."

Charlotte Bronte (1846–1855)

1. This week begin to have devotions or a quiet time each day. The "closet" time that is referred to in up-coming chapters is the time you take to be alone before the Lord. Each day, schedule a time to read your Bible, pray and worship God. The Bible study in each of the seven sections will take about ten to fifteen minutes per day.

2. "A girl's room is a much an expression of herself as her mother's house is an expression of herself." Together, take some

time and evaluate the daughter's room. Is it her castle, her den, her retreat? What are some ways Mother could help create that safe atmosphere? Look for inexpensive things to do together like stenciling or painting. Perhaps just re-arranging the room might make it more to her liking. Creating atmosphere does not have to be expensive. Present ideas to your husband/father and get his input

3. Create a budget for daughter's spending. For this, you don't need anything fancy. In a notebook, start by drawing lines for each category of spending. Total up what she earns in one month. Divide the money up into the categories she needs. For example: 10 percent to God, 30 percent to savings, 30 percent to clothing, 20 percent spending, 10 percent gift fund. Carefully record the income and expenditures in the appropriate columns throughout the month. At the end of the month, the daughter should evaluate her money management with her mother or father. It might be a good time to look into ways for the daughter to earn money. Moms, if you don't have a budget for your family, now would be a good time to set one up.

4. How much sleep do I need? How much exercise? What style of clothing is flattering? What does the family consider modest? What is not? Begin to discuss with and train the daughter on how to take care of the body in relation to sleep, diet and exercise. Daughter, make a date to go window shopping with Dad and/or Mom. Ask them what they considers modest and what they do not.

5. Educate yourself on money management and budgeting by getting some books from the library. Read them and apply what you think would work for your family.

❧ *Resources*

"FOR THE LITTLE WOMAN IS PASSING THROUGH A TRANSI-
TIONAL TIME IN HER DEVELOPMENT, AND SHE CAN
NOWHERE BE AS SAFE AND AS SHELTERED, AS IN THE SWEET
SECLUSION OF THE HOME."

Financial training products can be ordered on-line from:
www.crown.org, or by mail: Crown Financial Ministries P.O.
Box 2377 Gainesville, GA 30503-2377, (800) 722-1976.

Crown Financial Study for Teens Workbook by Larry Burkett

Teens love this study! Besides memorizing a key Scripture and
learning what God says about money, there is a practical exercise
at the end of each chapter to help teens create lifelong habits of
handling money responsibly. To order, call 1-800-722-1976.

Birth Order Book by Dr. Kevin Lehman

Are you the first-born, last, only or middle child? This book
will show you how your position in the family affects who you are
and what you choose to do with your life. Birth order also effects
your relationships with others, whether at home or on the job.
Available at www.christianbook.com.

Biography: Kept for the Master's Use by Frances Ridley Havergal

Almost every Christian at one time has sung the sweet hymn
of consecration by Frances Ridley Havergal: "Take My Life and
Let it Be." In this book, Frances discloses deep truths of complete surrender, what they meant to her and what they should
mean to us. Available at www.keepersofthefaith.com.

A Daughter at Home

Two

"A ROSEBUD SET WITH LITTLE WILFUL THORNS"

OT EVERY HOUSEHOLD IN THE LAND has its darling, ministering daughter, but no household is complete without one. Into what need of the hour does she not enter? What longing of the heart does she not fill? This dear young girl repeats in face and form the sweetness of the mother's past, and in trick and gesture, pose and accent, is a feminine copy of her father—the princess royal wherever we find her.

She becomes all the lovelier if she is gently guided. Encourage her not to be too subdued and restrained; as the charm of the rose is enhanced by its shielding briers, it is permitted to the daughter of the house to have in may minor details, her own way. If she notices alterations that could be made to make the house run more smoothly, they are made. If she desires innovations, her family sanctions them. Finally, the happy day of queenly prerogative has arrived, and her people, from the grandparents down, are her devoted and obedient subjects.

The mother in her chair of state is not often ready to abdicate merely because her little girl has let down her frocks, put up her hair and donned a young lady's attire in frills, ruffles, trains and laces and ribbons. Dear Mother prefers yet to keep the house in person and delegates only a small share to her daughters. But in portions of the homemaking, the girl naturally takes part, and especially is she in evidence in the home's hospitalities. She pours tea at five o'clock for the friends who informally call, and when the family has guests for supper she is there to help entertain the children. The small and graceful courtesies, never obtrusive but always appreciated, which add so much to a visitor's pleasure—the fresh towels in the guest chamber, the flowers renewed in bowl and vase, the bric-a-brac dusted, the slippers ready for Father's tired feet, the cushion softly interposed at the moment when Mother's back begins to ache, the prompting word which enables an aunt to tell her favorite story, the needles ready threaded for Grandmother—these little cares are within the province of the daughter of the house.

At this age she is learning tact. Hers is the happy knack of making people satisfied with themselves. The dear girl of fifteen can serve and be served by others in the family because she requests and does not order, and is unstinted in her pleasant return of thanks for their kindness. The correspondences she writes are examples that she knows what to say. In honeyed phrases, which commend her tact and discretion, she communicates to others. I am not surprised to find that, like Elizabeth Barret Browning's heroine in a familiar poem, "'Tis her thinking of others, makes you think of her," for the daughter of the house is truly an altruist.

Her father is proud of her growing beauty, her quick wit and her accomplishment. The bond uniting father and daughter is very subtle; it implies loyalty on the one side and courtliness on the other, and there is little in reason which he can deny her while she instinctively asks for what she wants with the air of one to whom half of the kingdom is already pledged. The two have much in common; they like the same amusements, they enjoy the same books and, when they go on a journey together, the father's attentions are clear for all to see. Outside, observe the relationship between the two and smile with approval.

Some skill should be developed by the girl in amateur "nursing," for there are often occasions when she may be called upon to care for illness and soothe an invalid. I am supposing that our girl herself is well, as every young woman should be, and that she prizes her health so that she does not foolishly overdraw her reserves. "I nursed my mother through two years of intense suffering," said a daughter, "and I was often with her at night as well as in the daytime, but I did not break down. I exercised regularly, and took what rest I could, and I kept cheerful for her sake." Lessons on first aid to the injured are beyond price, showing a girl what to do and how to do it in a case of emergency, when a person has had a fall, or is burned, or faints, or is wounded or maimed by an accident. Courses on babysitting and CPR are also part of invaluable preparation for the demands which sooner or later life will make upon her in the department of caring intelligently for the sick. This practical training and the time devoted to these skills will be put to good use and never wasted. If the daughter wishes to serve further in her day and generation, look for ways for her to serve in the church. Nursery duty, meals for shut-ins, teaching the little ones Bible stories, playing the piano or flute are all ways that her talents can be used by the Lord. Seeking ways to exercise the gift of serving is not vanity, but rather a proper way to serve!

I am supposing, dear rosebud of the little wilful thorns, that you are willing to bloom in the home borders, that you are not anxious for a wider career than home offers you. These are days of restlessness and aspiration beyond the bounds of home, and young women are invited on many sides to step into a sphere that seems wider than the somewhat circumscribed circle of home interests. A girl conscious of her own ability, with leanings toward professional business life, with the knowledge that she can successfully compete with others, may often say to herself, "Have I the right to fold my talent in a napkin; would I not be unfaithful and wasteful if I did not use it?" An ambitious and wide-awake young girl often chafes against the hampering conditions of her lot and wishes that she might, without question, do with her life as she pleases. In this she is not to be blamed, nor should she be hastily condemned. The point of view must be regarded and balanced with today's atmosphere and attitudes.

Over the past hundred years we have gone a long way forward. As far as women are concerned, the progress has been along lines of elevation and dignity. When, at twenty, a girl's friends began to speak of her as passé if, at that hour, no lover loomed up on the horizon, when she was kept in tutelage if unmarried long after she was a mature woman in years, experience and appearance, when "old maid" was a term of disrespect and a situation of reproach, it was not strange that some girls' only desire was to be married. Young women today may easily support themselves by their honorable endeavor, and their fathers and mothers no longer need for them a provision in marriage. If they marry, it is because their hearts go with the surrender of their hands, because love hallows the bond, not because they wish or need to be taken care of by a husband. The woman may care for herself. She need not be a burden for her toil-worn father, nor a clog upon her brothers since, if need be, she may herself become a wage earner.

This being conceded, may we not urge our thoughtful daughter that she shall continue on at home, taking these last few years left as a time to enjoy and prepare for her life outside the family home? The home at this time can be the most challenging place to learn and serve. At this time in a young girl's life she may be too self-conscious to bestow the loving word and the kind act. We will never be sorry for the moments of our self-effacement and our heedful thought for our beloved ones. Remember...

It isn't the thing you do, Dear,
It's the thing you leave undone
Which gives you a bit of heartache
At the setting of the sun.
The tender word forgotten,
The letter you did not write,
The flower you might have sent, Dear,
Are your haunting ghosts at night.

The home daughter who is not discontented with her lot but, on the contrary, is willing to accept her household, her people and her quiet post of service as the one God meant for her, will not find time hanging heavily on her hands. There is much room for tillage in the home vineyard. No background ever stands for so much to the conscientious young woman. Nowhere else can she find so many occasions for that lending hand which lightens every pack and so bravely helps the fellow pilgrim along on his journey to the heavenly city.

It is not merely an affair of putting a flower in the father's buttonhole, and mending the mother's laces, and making the desserts, and acting as a go-between when the soldiers in the camp are disgruntled. These little things count, but they are not all. Nor is it the singing of a song in the twilight, nor the playing of the sonata to listeners whose hearts keep time to the melody, those partial listeners who bore with small fingers when they beat time in their first lessons. This, too, is much, but not all.

It is being the mother's representative at any and every neighborly, social and church function which she cannot attend. It is taking her place when Mother is away from home. It is assisting the church when they need a piano player at a prayer meeting or service. It is the smoothing of a tangle among the young people. It is being young, and dear, and sweet, and well-poised and consecrating all you are to God. Surely, the home daughter need not fear to magnify her place of honor in God's world. And if she has moments of discouragement, as who has not, may she lean ever on the Friend who will always be at her side.

❧ *Mother to Mother*

"THE HOME AT THIS TIME MAY BE THE MOST CHALLENGING PLACE TO LEARN AND SERVE."

Glops of thick brown batter were spattered across the cluttered counter top. Dirty dishes lined the counter as if patiently waiting their turn to be washed. My little brown-haired girl, with flour smudged on her face, was attempting to be queen of the kitchen. Her scepter was the spatula, her cape, a kitchen towel. Her loyal subjects were eagerly waiting around the kitchen table for their queen to present them with fragrant rewards from the oven.

Mothers, do you remember the day when you started to hand over your domain to your daughter? For most of us, the years between fifteen and twenty will be the last few we have at home with our daughters before they enter the world. Training your daughter in domestic arts is both challenging and rewarding. In the next section, we be exploring the area of homemaking skills that will be important to your daughter if she marries or remains single.

❧ *Mother's Questions*

"A ROSEBUD SET WITH LITTLE WILFUL THORNS"

Mabel Hale (Beautiful Girlhood)

1. Ponder these questions and pen your answer in your journal. In what ways is your daughter like you? In what ways is she like your husband?

2. List some of the household tasks in which your daughter participates. Have you encouraged her to do so? If not, why?

3. Does your daughter participate in "amateur nursing" skills like helping when one has been injured in the family? What are some ways you could encourage her?

4. List some of the ways your daughter has served. In what other areas could she be encouraged to serve? In your church? In your community? In your family?

5. Thorns are the little pricks and sticks that are our self will. They are the things we don't want to do... just because. Take time to think about some of the "wilful thorns" you have encountered in your life. Write down what they were and how you were able to overcome them.

6. What are some your daughter has encountered? Perhaps they have included relationships in and out of the family, household tasks or service outside the home?

7. List some ways that she could overcome these obstacles. During your mentoring time with her, brainstorm ways she could overcome these thorns. Remember, half the battle is knowing and admitting that the obstacles are there.

❧ *Daughter's Questions*

"THORNS ARE THE LITTLE PRICKS AND STICKS THAT ARE OUR SELF WILL. THEY ARE THE THINGS WE DON'T WANT TO DO... JUST BECAUSE."

Anonymous

1. Simone De Beauvoir said, "...the daughter is for the mother at once her double and another person." Ponder this thought as you answer these questions in your journal. In what ways are you and your mother alike and and in what ways, different? In what ways are you like, or different from, your father?

2. List some household tasks you perform. Which ones do you particularly like or dislike? Which ones are you very good at? What new tasks would you like to learn (for example, bread baking, embroidery, ironing, sewing)?

3. "Amateur nursing skills" are skills you can always use whether you are married or single. How have you exercised these skills in your family? Record ways you have used such skills in the past. Are there ways you could improve them? How? Have you ever thought about pursuing a career in the medical field?

4. Service is a way to become involved in other people's lives while benefitting them. List different areas you have served in your family, neighborhood, church and community. In what areas do you feel "gifted" or especially successful?

5. In your own words, write out the definition of "wilful thorns." Make a list of the thorns that you have in your life right now, and how you can overcome them.

❧ *Bible Study*

"...SHOW ME YOUR FACE, LET ME HEAR YOUR VOICE; FOR
YOUR VOICE IS SWEET AND YOUR FACE IS LOVELY."

Song of Solomon 2:14b

Margaret Sangster wrote in the last sentence of Chapter Two, "...may she lean ever on the Friend who will always be at her side." One of the best, most effective ways to develop this friendship is to spend time with God in quiet time. Quiet time is a term used frequently in Christian circles. It refers to a time when you can draw away from your everyday life and the noisy world around you and seek to spend time with God. This time is more than just an appointment with God; it is the time that you get to talk with your best Friend, the One who loves you the most (Zeph. 3:17)!

How do you start? Certainly the best place to begin is in the beginning. Start by setting up a time when you can meet with your Lord. Early in the day is usually best. It is always best to meet with God before the busyness of the day crowds in. Start with fifteen minutes. Guard your time jealously! Do not allow other things to take away your time with Him. Increase the time you spend as the Lord leads. Make every attempt to accomplish this practice daily, when you are alone and can pray and talk to the Lord without self-consciousness. It is a habit that will change your life.

Where do you meet with God? Lovers often have a special place where they can be alone. Find or create a place where you can meet with the Lover of your soul. Perhaps your room, the porch, a spot in the garden or even in your closet would be best. Decide right now where you can best seek His face.

What is the goal of a quiet time? Philippians 3:10 gives us our goal: *"Know him (as a Person), and the power of his resurrection, and the fellowship of his sufferings, being made conformable to his death."* You want to know Him, but you also want to know how He sees you. Quiet time can be a time of self-examination, confessing and cleansing. You also want to know His thoughts and desires for you and your life. Developing a complete dependence on Him by bringing Him your need for wisdom, guidance, physical things and strength to meet temptations and problems is your goal (Isa. 40:29-31).

What should you do during a quiet time? The three main ingredients of quiet time are: the Word, prayer and meditation. In the resource section of this chapter, there is a form to help you mold your quiet time. Try to use it each time you study a passage of Scripture. This will help you record and keep track of your time with God. Here are some more suggestions for quiet time:

✤ To keep your thoughts from wandering, pray out loud. God loves to hear your voice (Song. Sol. 2:14)!

✤ Avoid getting into a rut by varying your routine.

✤ God has promised to be with you. Expect His presence (John 14:16; Matt. 28:20).

✤ Do not use this time to prepare for something else such as Sunday school, Bible study or any other thing that might "seem" worthy. This is your time with Him.

✤ Don't let it ruin your day if you miss your time with Him. If it is your fault, confess it to Him and accept His forgiveness (1 John 1:9).

Read the following verses and answer the questions.

1. Matthew 6:6 ~ According to this verse, what are the instructions and what is the benefit of praying to God in secret?

2. Matthew 26:36 ~ Where did Jesus go to pray?

3. John 4:23,24 ~ What kind of worship does God want from us? Define spirit. Define truth.

4. Isaiah 40:29-31 ~ List what the Lord gives to us when we go to Him. What does it mean to you to hope or wait on the Lord? List the benefits.

5. Joshua 1:8 ~ What did God promise Joshua? What was the condition? What does it mean to you to meditate on God's Word? Look up the word "meditate" in a dictionary.

6. As you spend quiet time with God you will learn many things. Read Psalm 139:17. How are you to react toward the thoughts and truths that are taught to you through the Holy Sprit? By recording this in a journal you can store up the treasure that you receive in your time alone with God.

In this last section there have been two suggestions to keep a record of the passages you study and the truths God reveals to you. They can be kept on the Daily Quiet Time form in the resource section at the end of this chapter and in your Bible Study Journal. For ideas on how to develop a quiet time system, refer to project five in this chapter.

❧ *Projects*

"THERE IS MUCH ROOM FOR TILLAGE IN THE HOME VINEYARD."

1. Make copies of the chore chart in the resource section of this chapter. Make chore assignments together that involve all the children in the family. The daughter could be the "adminis-

trative assistant" in the house. Her assignment could also be to do her chores well and make sure the other children get their jobs done well too. If there are problems, bring them to Mom and Dad because they are the authorities.

2. Develop a one-week menu plan. Create it by copying the Weekly Menu Plan in the resource section of this chapter. Note what the meals will be and who will prepare them. This is a good way to teach the value of nutritious meals and budgeting. Try creating the menus around supermarket specials. Give certain children the opportunity to cook some or all of the meals once or twice a week. By teaching/learning this skill now, you are training your daughter to be a good steward of time, money and resources.

3. Find out if your local college, school or fire department offers CPR and first aid classes. Take them together as a family project. Perhaps your daughter has an interest in the medical field. Attending these classes would be a way to "confirm" her calling.

4. Look for and provide service in your home, neighborhood or church. Perhaps you have an elderly neighbor or grandparent who would love a letter or a batch of muffins. Perhaps a young mother in your church needs some time out. By babysitting you could provide a much-needed service to her! Seek to serve and you will certainly find employment.

5. Develop a system to record your quiet time. One way is to obtain a three-ring binder. They come in a variety of colors and sizes. The Daily Quiet Time sheet, found in the resource section of this chapter, can be used as a lasting chronicle of what you have learned in your time with the Lord. Also include in your system lined paper to record your journal entries. Journal entries can be your response to certain Scripture passages that speak to you. Quotations are another thing that have a way of summing up what the Lord is saying. Other times, God uses the conversation

or teaching of others to confirm or point out things you need to work on. Record them! Another practice that I have found helpful is to write my prayers out in my journal, not just what I am praying for, but what I am praying as I go. Place these in a three-ring binder. Then, when you have your time with the Lord, you will have all you need to record your time together in one place.

❧ *Resources*

"BE IT EVER SO HUMBLE, THERE IS NO PLACE LIKE HOME."
John Howard Payne (1791–1852)

Bonnie's Household Organizer: The Essential Guide for Getting Control of Your Home by Bonnie Runyan McCullough

Bonnie's Household Organizer is an essential handbook for anyone! It offers workable systems to help achieve organization in your home, starting by showing you how to manage your time and tackle household clutter, by teaching you how to train your children, store things properly and improve work habits. It also offers ways to save money on food. Each chapter ends with practical ideas and applications. This was the first book I ever read on household management. I love it! Available at www.amazon.com.

The Family Manager by Kathy Peel

Kathy is a nationally known expert in family management and has now authored a year-round planner for women. The short cuts for wise shopping, kitchen work and speed cleaning are just a few of the ways she helps us organize our homes and lives. To order, call 1-800-247-4784.

Confessions of a Happily Organized Family by Deniece Schofield

This book gives lots of practical advice on how to have a neat house and calm mom, in a no-nag sort of way! Useable advice to make mornings, mealtimes and chores more fun and peaceful. Available at www.amazon.com.

Speed Cleaning by Jeff Campbell and the Clean Team

This humorous collection of quick tips and shortcuts was written by the owner of a cleaning service. Clean your entire house in forty-two minutes? YES! This book teaches you how to clean effectively so every move counts. Available at www.amazon.com.

Is There Life After Housework? by Don Aslett and Craig Lagory

Aslett takes the dread out of cleaning by teaching you the efficient methods and materials used by professional cleaners. Available at www.cleanreport.com.

Daily Quiet Time

"...SHOW ME YOUR FACE, LET ME HEAR YOUR VOICE; FOR
YOUR VOICE IS SWEET, AND YOUR FACE IS LOVELY."

Song of Solomon 2:14

Portion of Scripture: _____

Date: _____

1. Key verse:(memorize/meditate): _____

_____

_____

_____

2. Main teaching of the passage: _____

_____

_____

_____

3. Examples to follow: _____

_____

_____

_____

4. Errors to avoid: _____

_____

_____

_____

5. Truths or promises to claim: _____

_____

_____

_____

6. Commands to obey: _____

_____

_____

_____

7. How does this apply to my life? _____

_____

_____

_____

8. Action I can take? _____

_____

_____

_____

9. My prayer in light of this Scripture: _____

_____

_____

_____

_____

_____

_____

_____

_____

_____

_____

Weekly Menu Plan

"HE PROVIDES FOOD FOR THOSE WHO FEAR HIM; HE
REMEMBERS HIS COVENANT FOREVER."

Psalm 111:5

Week:	*Breakfast*	*Dinner*	*Supper*
Monday			
Tuesday			
Wednesday			
Thursday			
Friday			
Saturday			
Sunday			

Chore Chart

"WHATEVER YOU DO, WORK AT IT WITH YOUR WHOLE
HEART, AS IF WORKING FOR THE LORD..."

Colossians 3:24

Chore	Mon	Tue	Wed	Thu	Fri	Sat

Chore	Mon	Tue	Wed	Thu	Fri	Sat

* Write each child's chore in a certain colour
* Have older children check younger children's work
* Child needs to initial work when it is done
* Hang chart in central location like refrigerator

The Girl and Her Friends

Three

"SHARED JOY IS DOUBLED JOY, AND SHARED SORROW IS
HALF SORROW"

Swedish Proverb

THE ESSENTIAL TO PERMANENCE IN FRIENDSHIP
is unselfishness. To win and hold friends one
must be altruistic. A person may excite admi-
ration, may move to envy and may even exercise influence, without possessing the open
sesame which unlocks the heart of others and
invites the guest to enter and share in the treasures. Only sweet and true natures are endowed with the ability
for firm and enduring friendship; only those who love much
and therefore forgive much may expect to receive the same in
return. We have all known people who lavish material posses-
sions on others, yet they never seem able to make the recipient
love them. The utmost generosity did not awake a warmer feeling than a somewhat chilly gratitude. "The gift without the
giver is bare." We must pour out ourselves if we want to have
faithful and loyal friends, if we would find at every crisis and in
every exigency, a bodyguard of devoted followers to stand

staunchly at our side, for our defense, our protection and our
aid. Friendships from childhood are very sweet and sponta-
neous, but they are also frequently brief. Circumstances inter-
vene for separation, or as young people grow up they grow apart
by reason of different training and opposite social environment.
But sometimes they are made for life. The girl who sat beside
you at ten and looked over the same spelling buckwheat at
twelve, who shared your picnic lunch, and at fifteen lengthened
your dress, at twenty and at twenty-five continued to be your
dearest friend. In this case you will enjoy each other thoroughly
because you have a common fund of associations and memories.
You will know each other's thoughts before they are spoken and
understand one another's moods without the clumsiness of
explanation. No relationship is more ideal than that of two girls
who have grown up together, whose friendship strikes deep
roots into the soil of childhood.

Yet you who are leaving home today to spend the next four
years in a distant college, may be starting out to meet the most
uplifting, the most cheerful, the most congenial friend of your
whole life experience. You said goodbye to your mother with a
kiss and a long clinging embrace, on the porch of a farmhouse in
Maine. The other left her parents in a stately old colonial house
in Kentucky. Each of you, though you did not dream of it, was
to find in the other her counterpart, her companion, and bye and
bye, her best friend. When a girl has an intimate friend, or when
several girls form a group of congenial friends, there is no need
nor occasion for constant chattering about trifles nor for a great
deal of talk. They may speak or be silent; our friend is satisfied.
Just being together is enough to make us happy and contented.

A girl never permits herself to comment unfavorably upon
one friend to another. If she has a complaint to make, she car-
ries it in person to the individual whose attitude has puzzled her.

Loyalty is the life breath of real friendship. We hurt each other sometimes by our blunders, as when "our hard, unmeaning hands we thrust among the heart strings of a friend," but we never do this on purpose, nor do we discuss our friends and their shortcomings and infirmities with anyone under the sun. *"Bear ye one another's burdens"* (Gal. 6:2), is the inflexible law of friendship. Though estrangement between congenial friends may pass because of a meddling third party, it is almost impossible if the friendship is sincere, is based on the bedrock of Christian principle and is characterized by fairness and candor.

Sometimes older people smile at the sentimentality of the young, but this only occurs when the youth has waned from their own souls. What is sentiment? It is the sheen on the seashell, the perfume of the rose, the velvet smoothness on the roughened surface of the hill as you watch it in the evening light. When one loses the spontaneity of the child and the fresh enthusiasm of youth, when one's point of view becomes cynical or materialistic, then that person will scoff at the beautiful materialistic, then that person will scoff at the beauty of youthful friendships.

A girl's friends explain her even when she is a puzzle. If she chooses them carefully, if they are refined, cultivated, and lovely, she has herself the same qualities. The girls who are satisfied with loud-voiced, vulgar, and mean associates, condemn their own judgement, and label themselves as belonging to the lower caste. External situation of money, of dress, of expectations, of easy or hard fortune, have little or nothing to do with friendship which is founded on other things than these shifting conditions. It does not matter whether a friend lives in one room or in a great house, whether she is dressed well or plainly. Her clothing and her outside state are not parts of her. It does matter if she is well mannered, speaks in soft tones, uses good language and has good moral values. In our friends we desire people whose ways are similar to ours, whose values are the same. We want friends who comprehend our ambitions and sympathize in our efforts.

Girls may have among their friends a special friendship with their brothers and their friends. But it is by no means to be assumed that the bond of family makes you friends. Sisters are often the closest friends, but not always. Sisters and brothers may be devoted friends but may miss this great opportunity. A young man whose sister is his firm and congenial friend is armed against a multitude of evils. She is oftentimes able to discern and see problems and warn him before they occur.

Friendships between boys and girls are not always of the romantic nature. Far too often we spoil what might be a most delightful acquaintance between a young woman and a young man when we make the girl self-conscious by teasing her. A girl may have friends of the opposite sex on an equal footing, may give them of her cleverness and her quick intuition, may take from them strength and be aided by their clearness of vision, yet on neither side shall there be a suggestion of falling in love. Our Lord never said a sweeter word than, when addressing His disciples, He gave them a claim on His friendship: *"I have not called you servants, I have called you friends"* (John 15:15). To every young girl in the dawn of her life's day, the Master comes, offering friendship with Himself. Blessed is the heart that hears and responds, for to her will be given the hidden manna, the new name and the morning star.

❧ *Mother's to Mother*

"WE ARE TOGETHER, MY CHILD AND I, MOTHER AND CHILD, YES, BUT SISTERS REALLY AGAINST WHATEVER DENIES US ALL THAT WE ARE."

Alice Walker (1944–)

At one point, I sought my daughter for advice. I no longer remember what it was about. She asked questions to get a fuller picture of the situation and listened with empathy and careful consideration. At that point we made our first step toward friendship.

What a sweet treasure to have your daughter as your friend! In the next few years the relationship between you and your daughter will go through a transformation. You will make the journey that blessed mothers through the ages have made from mother to friend. The way may be easy or difficult, depending on the relationship you now have with your daughter. I cannot offer a map that will guide you to an ideal relationship, but I can direct you to the Mapmaker of your lives. Ask God for the wisdom and direction to proceed. In your time together, you will examine ways to choose friends, what a friend is, how to treat friends and, most importantly, your friendship with each other.

❧ *Mother's Questions*

"'BEAR YE ONE ANOTHER'S BURDENS,' IS THE INFLEXIBLE LAW OF FRIENDSHIP."

1. According to Margaret Sangster, "The essential permanence in friendship is unselfishness." Describe in your journal what it means to you to be unselfish in a friendship. What does it mean *for* you? What does it mean for your friend?

2. Give an example of how "the gift without the giver is bare." Explain how this may have occurred in your life or in the lives of others you have observed.

3. Think back to your best friend when you were growing up. What was her name? Describe how you met. What qualities made this person special to you? Are you still friends? Why or why not?

4. "A girl never permits herself to comment unfavorably upon one friend to another." This golden rule applies to women of all ages. Why could commenting on one friend to another cause problems? Are you guilty of this? Have you been a victim of this? What could you do to improve yourself on this matter?

5. Bearing one another's burdens is the inflexible law of friendship. Practically speaking, how can you bear your friend's burdens? Your daughter's? Your mother's? Relate in your journal and later discuss a time when your burdens were borne by a friend and the effect this had on your situation and you.

6. An old proverb states: "If you lie down with dogs you come up with fleas." How does this apply to friends? What kind of friends have you chosen in the past? What influence did they have on you? (By tactfully describing the negative influences in your life, you can teach your daughter to learn from your mistakes.)

7. Explain what kind of friendship you have with your brothers and sisters. Explore ways you could improve them.

8. Can boys and girls be friends without dating? Brainstorm for some fun activities that can be done without dating.

❧ *Daughter's Questions*

"A GIRL'S FRIENDS EXPLAIN HER EVEN WHEN SHE CAN'T
UNDERSTAND HERSELF."

1. According to Mrs. Sangster, "The essential permanence in friendship is unselfishness." Describe in your journal what it means to you to be unselfish.

2. Consider this old Swedish proverb: "A friend in need is a friend in deed." Have you ever had a friend in need? How did an unselfish friend help you or you her?

3. Think about your best friend. What is her name? Describe how you met. In your opinion, what qualities make her special to you? What does she do that makes you laugh? Evaluate your friendship. Is it unselfish? Why or why not?

4. Mrs. Sangster wrote, "A girl never permits herself to comment unfavorably upon one friend to another." Name some reasons you should follow this golden rule. Have you ever commented unfavorably about a friend? How could you have better handled that situation?

5. Describe some ways that you do, or might, bear a friend's burdens. Is it possible to bear burdens for your mother? Describe a time you have had your "burdens borne."

6. Discuss ways you could be friends with a boy without dating. Write down the pros and cons of having a friendship rather than a dating relationship.

❧ *Bible Study*

"A FRIEND LOVES AT ALL TIMES..."

Proverbs 17:17

If I want to know something about you, I would observe the kinds of friends you keep: those with whom you laugh, eat and spend your free time. The people you associate with are like a mirror of your soul. Friendships tend to have a life of their own, being, at times, unpredictable. Occasionally, you may lose friends because of distance, change or a broken relationship. Yet there is one friendship that will never change and always be available to you.

1. John 15:12-17 ~ On a copy of your Daily Quiet Time resource page, do a study on this passage. Read and meditate on these warm words of Jesus.

2. Read John 15:12-15 once again. Consider these questions:

  A. What is the greatest way to show others love?
  B. How do we practically do this?
  C. What must you do to be Jesus' friend?
  D. Have you chosen Jesus as your friend?

3. Read the following verses and note the warnings about "bad friendships": 1 Corinthians 15:33; 2 Corinthians 6:14-17; Proverbs 20:19, 22:24-25, 23:20-21, 29:24; Joshua 23:13; Judges 2:3; Psalm 26:4-5.

4. Matthew 5:23, 18:15 - This passage gives you the biblical way to react to problems that may occur in friendships. After reading it, list the steps outlined to restore the relationship. Try following these steps next time you have a problem with someone!

5. Memorize John 15:15.

6. Do you want to grow your faith? Start a prayer journal. It can be as simple as a notebook, loose-leaf paper in a binder or a book that has preprinted dates and Scriptures. Whatever mode you choose for your journal it needs to stand the trials of daily use. In your prayer journal you should include the contents of your prayer, the date and specific ways God answers your prayer. You also can keep your prayer list of people, events and situations you have chosen to pray about consistently. By keeping a prayer list, occasional forgetfulness can be overcome.

❧ Projects

"LET US BE GRATEFUL TO PEOPLE WHO MAKE US HAPPY; THEY ARE THE CHARMING GARDENERS WHO MAKE OUR SOULS BLOSSOM."

Marcel Proust (1871–1922)

1. Mothers and daughters, do you consider yourself friends? Explore how your relationship has changed over the last two or three years. How has it improved? Share with each other the areas you value about your friendship. Talk about the areas that you would like to improve on.

2. Daughters, make a list of your friends. Examine each friendship with your mother.

   A. What kind of friends have you been to one another?
   B. What are the weaknesses in your friendship?
   C. List some ways you could improve your side of the friendship.
   D. What are the ways you express your friendship? What are other ways you could show your friendship?

3. Read a book from the resource list on the different love languages together. Educate yourself on how others give and receive love and express friendship.

4. Read a book from the resource list on how young men and woman can be friends without dating. Talk about it as you read it. Ask questions, voice disagreements, talk about the ideas that make you think. These books are filled with good topics to discuss with each other.

❧ *Resources*

"A FRIEND IN NEED IS A FRIEND IN DEED."

Old Proverb

The Five Love Languages of Teenagers by Gary D. Chapman

At no other time in American history have parents, teachers and mentors been more desperate to find proven ways to reach teens. In response, best-selling author Gary Chapman presents *The Five Love Languages of Teenagers*. It contains practical guidance on how to discover and express the teen's primary love language—the way that he or she will best receive love. It is a tangible resource for stemming the tide of violence, immorality and despair engulfing many teens today. Available at www.lifetimebookandgifts.com.

The Bold Christian Youth Seminar by Jonathan Lindvall

This six-tape series scripturally challenges young people to higher standards than the world's:

- Radical commitment to Jesus
- Vision for your future ministry
- Faithfulness in the small things
- Honor—the key to the good life
- Humility—the key to favor
- Scriptural romance vs. dating
- Career decisions and preparation
- Further education
- Preparation for successful parenthood
- Foundation for financial freedom

For more information, contact: *Bold Parenting*, P.O. Box 820, Springfield, Ca 93265 (209) 539-0500.

Dating: Is it worth the risk? by Reb Bradley

This study was prepared for parents who want the best for their children and are open to the possibility that our present dating system is dangerous. Contact: *Family Ministries Publishing*, P.O. Box 1412, Fair Oaks, California 95628.

I Kissed Dating Goodbye by Joshua Harris

Are you tired of the game? Many teenage girls today feel discouraged that they do not have a boyfriend. Harris encourages the reader to look at their own character rather than being caught up in the infatuation that surrounds and defines dating. It is a challenge to regard love as a selfless act, in line with the Word of God, rather than a feeling one can fall into and out of. Contact: Questar Publishers, Inc., P.O. Box 1720, Sisters, Oregon 97759.

When God Writes Your Love Story by Eric and Leslie Ludy

Eric and Leslie are a powerful voice to their generation. As full-time speakers, writers and musicians, they challenge and encourage young adults and singles around the world to pursue holiness in every aspect of their lives. Available at www.christianbooks.com or call 1-800-247-4784 to order.

Four

Her Innocent Pleasures

"LIFE HOLDETH MUCH HAPPINESS. A DAY IS LIKE A GOLDEN CUP, WHICH GOD HIMSELF STOOPED DOWN TO BLESS, BEFORE HE FILLED IT UP."

 HUNDRED YEARS AGO THE YOUNG GIRL found waiting for her a great variety of household tasks that we are free from today. Modern convenience has made a wonderful forward stride in this hundred years. Our houses in their heating and lighting, from furnace to air conditioner, have freed us from an immense amount of hard work. It used to be that loaf sugar and rock salt were pulverized by hand for household use, while the flax of the fields and and the wool of the flocks were spun and woven by women of the family on their domestic looms. Every culinary process involved threefold the time and care that the task at present demands. Journeys were by stagecoach or sloop instead of car, train, and bus. All the nice things like jellies, jams and preserves were prepared in the home kitchen by the mother and her daughters and maids. Young woman had more to do with housework than they can possibly

have now. However, it would be an error to believe that household work and management does not require some time, thought and effort to be invested by the household executive of today.

It would be an inaccuracy to fancy that our great-grandmothers and their daughters had no pleasures. They were social, and they had brilliant parties where the gentlemen were devoted and the ladies were gracious. A fine, old-school courtesy prevailed. Manners, though elaborate and formal, did not prevent what every youth longs for—a good time. Yet the girls of that bygone period were less fortunate than ours are. Many a willowy damsel fainted and pined away and was laid in her grave, all on account of a foolish vanity which urged her to compress her lungs and crush her waist into the semblance of an hour glass; many held to the silly notion that their shoes had to be pretty and not sensible.

I am glad that the women of today have feet shod with sensible, sturdy shoes that fit them and that corsets are no longer an instrument of torture. No girl who reads this page has ever gone to a party with nine stiff petticoats tied around her waist, but many of your great grandmothers went to church in skirts that stuck out and rattled with an abundance of starch. A girl of the past might ride on horseback, seated on her own pony, or behind her father or brother. She might have taken long walks, and sometimes she did and she could drive, row a boat, and work in her garden. Today, girls play basketball, tennis, soccer and golf. They freely engage in most sports that young men excel at. Today's girls are taller than their predecessors, and quite often outgrow their mothers by an inch or two. Their hands and feet, though well proportioned, are larger than was once fashionable. We have learned that life means service, and service must have its fit equipment in a clear head and healthy body. Innocent pleasures for girls include much outdoor exercise and freedom.

Every girl should, so far as she can, secure and set apart a part of each day for the development of her body. Perfect health is within reach of most of us, if we will but strive for it. But it is also true that just as nature enjoys rest after duty, a girl's body also needs sufficient time to rest.

Among your innocent pleasures are you willing to include that lost art of sewing? Whether it be sewing with a machine to make clothing or household adornments or by hand to embroider tea towels, pillow cases or needlepoint and counted cross stitch, to a girl who likes her needle there may be hours of great enjoyment as she sits cozily with her mother and sisters on long sunny mornings or quietly ebbing evenings while the flow of talk goes smoothly on.

A knack with pencil and brush and skill with the camera are among the pleasures worth cultivation. A visit, a jaunt, a trip abroad or an excursion at home will be made doubly interesting and attractive if souvenirs of its peculiar features are brought back in an amateur artist's portfolio. One needn't aim at effects which only the most accomplished artist can attain. When one sketches from memory, for personal satisfaction, the scenes and situations are put down on paper to make the journey memorable.

Developing a habit of writing in your journal or diary is another way to preserve the moment. One woman said she wrote down the events in her life so she could savor them. The enjoyable memories take on a lasting hue when recorded in a journal.

A girl should cultivate a gift of simple cookery so that planning, shopping and preparation may not be beyond her skill. Many a young wife received a shock when she was expected to shop economically and prepare tasty meals for the first time in her life for her new husband. Dear girl, now is the time for you to practice and become well trained in menu planning and cooking a variety of different dishes.

Food is for the nourishment of our body but is can also be a time where the family can bond by engaging in an enjoyable experience together. For example, candy making is by no means a difficult art, and a great deal of fun may be had over fudge and taffy. Every girl must know how to make a cup of tea. There is no mystery in this, since the scalding of the pot, the fresh boiling of the water, and the infusion of the tea for two minutes and no more are all simple and easy to be remembered. On their observance success depends.

Food preparation and entertaining go hand-in-glove. In the 1830s it was customary for a young woman to receive her friends in her mother's parlor in the evening, while the mother did her mending in the dining room or in her own bedroom. Today, the family stays together when a caller happens by. The presence of the parents doesn't seem to act as a handicap on the spirits of the young people. And their friends are open to having an enjoyable evening.

God means us to be happy. He has spread beauty broadcast over the earth and made this a lovely world sweet with music and radiant with stars by night and sunshine by day. If we are depressed and gloomy there must be something wrong!

Now and then a girl is very sensitive or overly conscientious. She distresses herself over imagined slights or broods over her own errors and faults. This is not the best way, nor in it is there the least element of the praiseworthy. Our self-love, our personal vanity, is wounded and we imagine injustices and criticisms which were never meant. We loom too largely in our own thoughts; we may as well own that we are more interesting to ourselves than we should be. Blessed is the girl whose mind is not occupied with the impression she is making, who exacts little and is grateful for every attention, while asking no favors. A most unhappy girl is she who indulges in fits of the blues and refuses to recognize any brightness unless self is in the middle of it. This kind of temperamental behavior is as much a matter of regret as a blemish on her skin.

About our sins, our shortcomings, our forgetfulness of God, our neglect of plain duty—they are to be repented of in the closet. The closet is the secret hour of communion. Let us tell them in the ear of our Savior and, in deep humility and earnest contrition, ask for pardon. The merciful Savior never denies us forgiveness, nor does He wish us to go on mourning over sin forgiven. We must learn to carry our burdens to the cross, but it is our privilege to bear a song away. "Let little sharp vexations And the briers that catch and fret, Let us take them all to the Helper, Who has never failed us yet."

Every one of us owes it to herself and her generation to learn to become a light-bringer. Do you remember Robert Browning's poem in which Pippa passes a little hard-working peasant who has only one holiday in the long year and, as she goes singing by, sin withers at the sound of her voice, sorrow is soothed and love grows strong and pure? Pippa passes, a little thankful maiden, and life is richer because of the maid's unconscious benediction. Ah, dear girls, be happy, be sweet, be good. "God's in His Heaven All's right with the world."

❧ Mother to Mother

"LIFE HOLD MUCH HAPPINESS."

"Many hands make the load light!" said the sweet, thickly-accented voice of my German grandmother as we were clearing the table. Even thirty years later that very phrase whisks me back into the warm, cozy kitchen that smelled of strong coffee and

freshly baked pumpernickel. Grandma taught me of her innocent pleasures by working with me. Whether it was pounding
down the mountain of fragrant dough, swishing hot water
around in the tea pot in preparation for the afternoon tea time
or the "knit one, pearl one" of her needle clacks, her warm arms
encircled me, her hands on mine.

Her attitude of working and playing together was not only
contagious, it was lasting! The motto, "Many hands make the
load light!" can still be heard in my house. Mothers, you have
not only the responsibility of teaching your daughters how to
work, but the privilege of showing her ways to enjoy life with
simple, innocent pleasures. If this is an area you have not given
consideration, I encourage you to examine your life and the way
you place times of enjoyment in your day. Look for opportunities to explore innocent pleasures with your daughter.

❧ *Mother's Questions*

"'LIFE'S SIMPLE PLEASURES ARE THE BEST, ALL THE LITTLE
THINGS THAT MAKE YOU SMILE AND GLOW, ALL THE THINGS
YOU KNOW."

VanCamp's Bean Jingle

1. In your journal, describe some of the domestic challenges
your grandmother or mother talk about. Consider how much
life has changed and the conveniences that give you more time.
Share your memories with your daughter.

2. Have you set an example of taking time each day to care for
your body? Do you take time to rest, exercise, eat a balanced diet,
read the Word of God? What areas do you need to improve on?

How could you create time for this? What are areas your daughter could improve on? List them and brainstorm for ways to make certain you both have the time to do these important things.

3. What are some of your innocent pleasures? What about these activities gives you pleasure? Picture yourself enjoying one of them. How does this activity make you feel? Describe the feelings in your journal. Do you know your daughter well enough to know what activities she enjoys?

4. Over the past four weeks you have been developing the habit of journal-keeping. Has this become one of your innocent pleasures? Do you find yourself enjoying recording your thoughts, or dreading it?

5. Reflect on how your family treats your daughter's friends. Ask for your husband's views on the friendships and how you might improve on them. In your journal, describe how you would like your daughter's friends to behave and interact with the family. If possible, take steps to make it happen.

6. Margaret describes a girl is caught in a great amount of introspection. I call this a case of "ingrown eyeballs." This malady occurs when we "loom too largely in our own thoughts." All of our thoughts are focused on our needs, wants, problems and desires. Mother, are you afflicted with this condition? Is your daughter? Comment in your journal why this is not beneficial.

❧ *Daughter's Questions*

"EVERY ONE OF US OWES IT TO HERSELF AND HER GENERATION TO LEARN TO BECOME A LIGHT-BRINGER."

1. Formulate your thoughts on how modern conveniences have effected your life and record them in your journal. Has the

modern way of doing things been for our good or has it been for evil? Try to give reasons and examples for each.

2. If you could live in any time period, which would it be and why? Evaluate what reasons would attract you. Would it be for adventure, discovery, comfort or to witness some historic event?

3. Margaret wrote, "Every girl should set apart a time each day for the development of her body." Is this a habit of yours? How could you incorporate this into your life? Explain why this habit would benefit you.

4. What are some of your "innocent pleasures"? What about these activities gives you pleasure? Picture yourself enjoying one of them. How does this activity make you feel? Describe this feeling and the experience in your journal. Do you know what some of your mother's favorite activities are? If not, find out.

5. Having friends in your home as guests is one of the pleasures Margaret mentions. Reflect on and record the manner in which your family gets along with your friends. List some ways your family could improve on this.

6. Occasionally, a young girl "looms too largely in her own mind." Are you guilty of this? Reflect on some ways that you could correct and avoid this.

❧ Bible Study

"THE LORD IS NEAR TO ALL WHO CALL HIM, TO ALL WHO CALL ON HIM IN TRUTH."

Psalm 145:18

One innocent pleasure that reaps eternal rewards is prayer. Prayer affirms, cultivates and enriches your relationship with

God while He speaks to you and guides you in the way He wants you to go. God longs to have that fellowship with you in prayer (see John 4:23). It seems almost unbelievable that the Creator would want to have a friendship with the creation. And yet, that is what God wants.

1. Luke 11:9 and 10 ~ Using your Daily Quiet Time resource page, delve into the meaning and application of this for your life.

2. Go to the resource section of this chapter and photocopy a Prayer and Action page. One way of getting to know God is to find out what He thinks and desires through His Word. Describe a situation in the "ask" section, "seek" out what God says in His Word and record it. Then record the action you plan to take in the "knock" section. Be certain that the actions you take are in line with what Scripture says. Read Luke 11:9 and 10.

3. Start keeping a weekly record of your prayers. Fill out at least three things you would like to pray about. Record how the Lord answers your prayers.

Suggestions: In a three-ring binder, organize your quiet time resources according to the following pattern—one Prayer and Action page per week, six quiet time pages per week and three lined pages for journalling your spiritual insights, written prayers, Bible promises, etc.

Prayer is more than "getting" God to do things for you. Prayer is "letting" Him do things through yourself and others. It is allowing God to conform your attitude to be like His.

4. Read the following verses and record what God is teaching you about prayer: Ephesians 6:18; Jeremiah 29:13; Proverbs 15:8,29; Isaiah 59:1,2; Psalm 37:4,5; Hebrews 4:14, 11:6; Matthew 6:6,7, 7:7-11.

5. Memorize Matthew 7:7-11.

❦ *Projects*

"FILL YOUR PAPER WITH THE BREATHINGS OF YOUR HEART...."
                                    William Wordsworth (1770–1850)

1. Find a simple sewing pattern and learn how to use a needle or a machine. Or choose and purchase a craft-store kit that teaches you how to cross stitch, embroider or applique. This craft can develop into gifts to give or even a business to start.

2. Purchase a sketch pad and begin filling it with illustrations of your life. The moments captured in your drawings with a brief description in your prettiest handwriting will long be treasured. Or work at developing that handwriting into calligraphy, a discipline that will give both pleasure and long service. How about putting the family's photo collection into a memory book? Or create a book of heirloom pictures for your family's history.

3. Television is one of the most common and subtle time thieves. For one week, monitor the amount of time you watch television. Multiply this by four and then by twelve. In this way you will be able to estimate the approximate number of hours you would spend in one year watching TV. Does this number shock you? Try getting control of the "one eyed monster" by setting up viewing times and limiting the number of hours spent. When you do this, use the saved time for some family fun or encourage individual growth by reading or developing a new hobby.

4. Look at the calendar and plan a family fun night. Invite another family or families over for a night of games and candy making. See our resource page for some "family night" recipes. Bring the extra to your neighbors and shut-ins.

5. A simple cup of tea can make an ordinary happening an experience! During your times spent in Bible study and discus-

sion, cultivate the old custom of "tea time." Make a pot of tea using the directions in the resource section. Use your prettiest china cups and saucers and get out the linen napkins. Both of these niceties will make the time spent even more memorable.

6. Start a journal today if you haven't already. *Stepping Heavenward*, by Elizabeth Prentiss, is a inspiring example of a girl's journal kept from age sixteen to her grown-up years. It will encourage you to step heavenward, to live with great humility, tranquility, hope and greater godliness. This can be a great inspiration for what journalling can be. A journal is different than a diary. In a diary, one records daily events. A journal is used to record not only events, but how they effect you. It can be used to process and find meaning in your life. It can also be used to record Scripture, Bible promises or truths you have learned. It can be a place to record a quotation that means something to you or a conversation God has used in your life. Take up the innocent pleasure of journalling and you will reap the rewards all of your life.

❧ *Resources*

"THANK GOD FOR TEA! WHAT WOULD THE WORLD DO WITHOUT TEA? HOW DID IT EXIST? I AM GLAD I WAS NOT BORN BEFORE TEA."

Sydney Smith 1779-1845

Tea by the Pot

Here are a few hints on how to make a pot of tea!

❧ Fill the kettle with cold water not warm. Cold water contains oxygen bubbles that make for a better cup of tea.

❧ Pour water into the pot immediately after it has boiled. Water that has boiled for a long time has a flat taste.
❧ Choose a tea of high quality for best results.
❧ Pack tea ball with loose-leaf tea. Allow some room so the leaves can expand as they become wet.
❧ Use a silver, pottery, or ceramic tea pot when making tea. Aluminum or enamel-coated pots will spoil the flavor.
❧ Remember, if your pot of tea is too strong, water can be added to dilute it.

Fantastic Fudge

3 cups sugar
3/4 c. butter or margarine
2/3 c. evaporated milk
12 oz. pkg. semi-sweet chocolate pieces
7 or 10 oz. jar marshmallow cream
1 c. chopped nuts (optional)
1 tsp. vanilla

Combine first three ingredient in 2 1/2 qt. saucepan. Bring to full, rolling boil, stirring constantly. Boil for 5 minutes over medium heat, stirring constantly. Remove from heat. Add chocolate and stir until melted. Add the rest of ingredients. Beat until well blended. Pour into greased 9 x 13-inch pan. Makes 3 delicious pounds of Fantastic Fudge!

Old Fashioned Taffy for Pulling

2 c. sugar
1/2 c. water
1 c. white syrup
1 T. vinegar
1 tsp. vanilla

1 T. butter
1/4 tsp. soda

Cook sugar, water, syrup and vinegar until a hard ball is formed when a teaspoon full is put in a cup of cold water. Remove from heat; add vanilla and butter. Add soda; stir well. Pour into buttered cake pan. When slightly cool, pull until taffy pulls white.

"PLEASURE IS A BY-PRODUCT OF DOING SOMETHING THAT IS WORTH DOING."

A. Lawrence Lowell (1874–1925)

Drawing Textbook by Bruce McIntyre

This guide is a teaching tool that contains 222 drawing exercises. The exercises give you practice and teach the seven key elements of drawing and alignment. Each simple lesson comes with a step-by-step explanations. Available at www.lifetime-bookandgifts.com or call 1-800-377-0390 to order.

Calligraphy Kit by Usborne

This set gives pictures that enable one to master the art of calligraphy. Learn a creative skill that you can use over and over again. Available at www.christianbook.com.

Fun with Origami by John Montroll

Beginners can master the simple shapes of a sailboat, jet plane, and paper cup, while intermediate paper crafters can make a bird, whale fish and penguin. Explains and diagrams 17 projects according to difficulty. Available at www.amazon.com.

Easy Carpentry Projects for Children by Jerome Leavitt

Instructions for making fifteen different projects from wood, with information on materials and tools and general directions for any woodworking project. Available at www.amazon.com.

How to Draw and Paint Animals in Pencil, Charcoal, Watercolor by Linda Birch

Learn to master the art of drawing and painting animals. Offers suggestions for quickly capturing a moving animal in sketches. A plethora of information for the budding artist. Available at www.amazon.com.

Complete Guide in Sewing: Step-By Step Techniques for Making Clothes and Home Furnishing by *Reader's Digest*

A perfect book for providing sewing fundamentals and the use of up-to-date equipment. This book even teaches you how to choose fabrics so you can create professional-looking clothes. Available at www.amazon.com.

Prayer and Action

Ask *and it will be given to you*	Seek *and you will find*	Knock *and the door will be opened to you*
Write your request	*Record Scripture*	*Action you will take*

Her Books

Five

"WE GET NO GOOD BY BEING UNGENEROUS EVEN TO A
BOOK."

N INTIMATE AND WIDE ACQUAINTANCE
with books is a work that will take a
lifetime. Most young women under
twenty have not had time to read very
much, though it is a great advantage to
them to have read a little. Schools and
colleges act as guideposts along the
roads to the treasure houses of literature. Ideally, they teach what
to read and what to pass by. A young girl should be introduced
during her school days to some of the most distinguished histo-
rians, dramatists and poets of her own tongue and have acquired
some knowledge of Shakespeare, Milton, Pope, Wordsworth,
Browning and Tennyson. A good, well-rounded introduction to
English, Dutch, Spanish and American history needs to be had.
She needs to have some idea of who Carlyle, Ruskin, Pater and
Thoreau are. By having read the best, she has some discernment
as to why it is the best.

Frankly, if she would admit her preference, unless she is a student born and bred, she will tell you that for pleasure she chooses a good novel. Here there is wide room for selection of topics or time periods. No one is obligated to waste an hour today over a worthless or wicked book because there are so many good books to choose from. The well-read girl has encountered Jane Austen and is surprised to discover that her heroines, except for a change of costume, fit very easily into twenty-first-century grooves. The wonderful Bronte sisters, writing their fiery romances from the subdued atmosphere of the Yorkshire moors, have revealed to her what genius can do unaided by fortunate accessories and have led her to the study of their lives. Discovering facts about an author's life always makes their work more interesting. *Wuthering Heights, Jane Eyre* and *Villette* are all illuminated when one reads what manner of education, what style of friendship and what home bringing-up the gifted daughters of Patrick Bronte had. The ordinary young woman does not feel obligated today to read Sir Walter Scott yet, lacking familiarity with his work, she cannot claim to be educated in English literature. Even though what was once a fascination may assume the guise of a task, she must read the Waverley novels, and submit herself to the spell of Scott's lyrical muse; read "Marmion," "Lord of the Isles" and "Lady of the Lake."

If, in childhood, so many were not spoiled by reading stories and childish tales which simply amuse us without requiring mental effort, there would be more girls to enjoy books to which the compliment of attention must be paid. A multitude of childish books is a misfortune to children, though fairy tales are a good diet for young and old because they cultivate the imagination, a royal gift of God which we cannot too highly value. The young girl must not overlook Dickens, Thackeray,

George Eliot and William Black, though she need not read every one of their works. *A Tale of Two Cities, Little Doris, David Copperfield* and *Bleak House* will give her the freedom of the Dickens' land; *The Virginians, Henry Esmond, Fair and the Newcomes* are masterpieces of that marvelous writer and magnificent man, William M. Thackeray, and she may read them more than once. From the shelf of George Eliot's work she may choose a good and impressive array. A few of her titles are *Daniel Deronda, Middlemarch*, and *Adam Bede*. Some of William Black's works include *The Princess of Thule, Macleod of Dare* and *A Daughter of Heth.*

Among current writers of fiction, seek wise advice before you devote precious time to their study. Some ways to find good books are to find a book list that has suggested reading for your age level or on specific time periods. You could ask your mother what books she has read and would approve of you reading. A book has as an immediate effect and as far-reaching an influence upon the receptive mind, as a bad companion; sometimes it makes a more indelible impression than any other bad companion can make.

On a girl's own bookshelf in her own room, what shall we find? Probably the books she loves best. First and most important, her Bible. I hope we shall see a worn Bible, one which bears evidences of being often read. Then, perhaps, a book of favorite daily devotions. It is like some sweet and lovely flower for every day picked from a great garden where grows herbs of many flavors and trees of the Lord's own planting. She will have a school book or two, a story she has loved, a memoir she has found helpful. If there are two or three missionary biographies or a few books on travel and adventure, I would guess that she appreciates valor and heroism and takes an interest in the outside world. Her books will indicate her tastes and her character. They will show where she browses for her daily food; they will describe character as unerringly as a camera captures a face. A well-furnished mind is like a beautifully appointed home; it has room for many things and must be kept with constant vigilance. Moth and rust mar and ruin the house in which no one lives. Simple neglect is more destructive than continual use. We often meet women who have ceased to grow because they have ceased to study, having ceased to be receptive and responsive. By forming the habit of reading and arranging for an hour with a good book in the day's work, every woman, young or older, will increase her mental wealth and her facility to learn. A girl's greatest charm in not in her graceful figure nor a beautiful grace; it is in her power to interest those whom she meets. To be an interesting woman one must have a bright and wide-awake mind. She must use her talents that they will increase. It is eternally true that to him that has, and exercises the gifts, more shall be given, while from him that has and does not use the gifts, there shall be a loss.

I had a beautiful garment
And I laid it by with care;
I folded it close, with lavender leaves,
In a napkin fine and fair;
"It is far too costly a robe," I said,
"For one like me to wear."

So never at morn or evening
I put my garment on;
It lay by itself, under clasp and key,
In the perfumed dusk alone,
Its wonderful broidery hidden
Till many a day had flown.

There were guests who came to my portal,
There were friends who sat with me,
And, clad in soberest raiment,
I bore them company;
I knew that I owned a beautiful robe
Though its splendor none might see.

There were poor who stood at my portal,
There were orphaned sought my care;
I gave them tenderest pity,
But had nothing beside to spare;
I had only the beautiful garment,
And the raiment for daily wear.

At last on a feast-day's coming,
I thought in my dress to shine;
I would please myself with the luster
Of its shifting colors fine;
I would walk with pride and marvel
Of its rarely rich design.

So out from the dust I bore it—
The lavender fell away—
And fold on fold I held it up
To the searching light of day.
Alas! The glory had perished.
While there in its place it lay.

Who seeks for fadeless beauty
Must seek for the use that seals
To the grace of a constant blessing,
The beauty that use reveals.
For into the folded robe alone
The moth with its blighting steals.

Girls, may I remind you to read your Bibles? Not merely a few hurried lines in the early morning and a few verses at night when you are half asleep, but, with listening ear and with a reverent eye, realizing that you are in God's presence and that He is speaking to you, read the divine Word. Do not omit the Old Testament, nor forget the New; the one is the following out of the other and the two are interdependent. Nor read to criticize; rather come to the Book as they who are thirsty come to a well, as they who are weary, to a pillow, as they who are afraid, to a refuge. Learn the Bible by heart, whole chapters of it, and be assured the day will come when the precious bits of truth will be to you as the fine gold and the fadeless gem. Choose where you will: the whole Bible is God's inspired message to humanity and you cannot read a single book without profit. Whatever other literature is noble, this is nobler. Whatever else be full of sweetness and light, this Book of God surpasses it. It is as a lamp on a dark night, as a brook in the desert, as a flower in the fallow field, as a star in the sky.

With other books, you may safely trust yourself to take up the reading at odd moments or when you have time to fill. But the Bible should not be left to when the mood strikes you. It should be read seriously and at a stated time or times in your day. The morning seems to be a time that works well for most. Before the business of the day intrudes, while you are still rested after sleep, sit down for a little while and listen to God's message to you. Read the Book before you pray and you will be able to pray with its counsel fresh in your mind. Make the daily closet service a habit not to be lightly broken, and do not leave your closet until you have read your chapter or your few texts if you have time for no more. Take a verse with you each morning as your motto for the whole day. Meditate by considering that particular verse and how it illumines your life. The Book is meant to give us our marching orders.

❧ *Mother to Mother*

"NO ONE IS OBLIGED TO WASTE AN HOUR TODAY OVER A
WORTHLESS OR A WICKED BOOK."

"Can we read just one more chapter?" my five-year-old
daughter pleaded. Together we had embarked on the adventure
of reading "chapter books." *Charlotte's Web* opened the door
these lengthier works. Each evening before bed I would nestle
my children around me and read a chapter or two from this
book. The world opened as our imaginations propelled us to far-
away places while cuddling under the warm covers at home.
Together we entered the domain of Narnia and uncovered a
treasure chest of spiritual truths. We climbed Switzerland's
mountains and hid in attics from the Nazis. We were catapult-
ed through time and space, book after book. We laughed until
we cried at the antics of *Hank the Cowdog* and the author's
description of the everyday life of a cowdog. The memories of
travels and experiences created in our reading time are as indelible as the ink on the pages we read.

Even though all four of us cannot comfortably fit into one
bed today, I still have the privilege of reading to my children.
Looking back over the years I see the importance of encourag-
ing them to read. Perhaps one of the greatest legacies I gave my
daughter and sons was the love of good books.

Wise Solomon wrote, *"Of the making of books, there is no
end"* (Eccl. 12:12). How true this is today! There seems to be no
end to the amount of information and literature available to us.
Some books are worth our time and some are certainly not.
Ladies, what are your standards for good reading material? How
do you judge whether a book is a worthy companion and friend

for your daughter? For yourself? How do you plan to teach your daughter to choose worthy books? In the following sections you will be encouraged to explore the world of books with your daughter and hopefully set a standard for choosing good and appropriate reading material.

❧ *Mother's Questions*

"'A WELL-FURNISHED MIND IS LIKE A BEAUTIFULLY APPOINTED HOME."

1. Do you enjoy reading? What kind of books do you prefer? Would you allow your daughter to read them? Recall and tell your daughter about the kind of books you liked to read when you were fifteen.

2. Fairy tales are said to cultivate your "royal gift from God," your imagination. Do you still have your gift? If so, how are you using it? Examples might be in decorating your home, supervising a family picnic or creating a gorgeous quilt. If not, what are ways you could recapture this lost blessing?

3. "A book has as immediate an effect and as far reaching an influence upon the receptive mind as a bad companion; sometimes it makes a more indelible impression than any other bad companion can make." Why do you think books can reach and influence a receptive mind as much as bad companions? List and give reasons to support your opinion.

4. At this time in your daughter's life, do you feel a responsibility to help guide her in choosing books? Or do you feel that would be censorship? What are some ways you could gently guide her in her book choices?

5. Read the poem in Chapter Five out loud to your daughter. What warnings does it contain? Is there an example to follow? To avoid? How are you like the main character? How are you different?

6. Is your mind "bright and wide awake" or has it ceased to dream, learn and grow? Explore and create an action plan for ways to revitalize your mind. For example, find a book list and start to read the "classics." Start memorizing Scripture. Learn a new language. Develop a new hobby. Find an interest and learn all you can about it.

7. Honestly explore your feelings about reading God's Word. Recall a time when the precious gem of God's Word was a refuge or a guide to you. Record it in your journal.

♣ *Daughter's Questions*

"A GIRL'S GREATEST CHARM IS NOT IN HER GRACEFUL FIGURE, NOR A BEAUTIFUL FACE; IT IS IN HER POWER TO INTEREST THOSE WHOM SHE MEETS."

1. Do you read for enjoyment? Describe why you do or do not delight in reading.

2. Describe a recent time when you used your "royal gift from God," your imagination. Perhaps you used it to play with your younger brothers and sisters, or perhaps you were indulging in a daydream. If you want, write it down in your journal with as much detail as possible.

3. "A book has as immediate an effect and as far reaching an influence upon the receptive mind as a bad companion; sometimes it makes a more indelible impression than any other bad companion can make." Reflect on why you believe this state-

ment could be true. List qualities your family would consider appropriate and inappropriate in books you read.

4. Think about and examine how you would feel if your mother and father were to guide you in your book choices. Compare your feelings to what the Bible says about obeying your parents "in the Lord." Discuss with your mother and father the books they would encourage you to read.

5. Proverbs 24:3-5 states:

> *By wisdom a house is built, and through understanding it is established; through knowledge its rooms are filled with rare and beautiful treasures. A wise man has great power, and a man of knowledge increases strength.*

Take a moment and imagine your mind as a beautifully furnished house. What actions could compare to filling the room with rare and beautiful treasures? What would compare to keeping it with constant vigilance? For example, dusting rooms might be compared to looking for and sweeping away impure thoughts; cleaning windows might be like washing your heart with the Word of God.

6. Review and list ways you can use God's Word in your life. Recall and write about a time when the "precious gems" of the Word were to you a refuge and a strength. If you have never used God's Word in this manner, look for ways to actively apply it to your life!

❧ *Bible Study*

"O GIVE ME THAT BOOK!" AT ANY PRICE GIVE ME THE BOOK OF GOD! HERE IS KNOWLEDGE ENOUGH FOR ME."

John Wesley (1703–1791)

Look up the following verses to discover who wrote the Bible: 2 Timothy 3:16; 2 Peter 1:20-21. The Bible is the very Word of God! It is communication from God to you for absolutely every situation in your life. It is living, active and sharp (Heb. 4:12). Read this verse:

> *The law of the Lord is perfect, reviving the soul; the testimony of the Lord is sure, making wise the simple; the precepts of the Lord are right, rejoicing the heart; the commandment of the Lord is pure, enlightening the eyes; the fear of the Lord is clean, enduring forever; the ordinances of the Lord are true, and righteous altogether. More to be desired are they than gold, even much fine gold; sweeter also than honey and drippings of the honeycomb. Moreover by them is thy servant warned; in keeping them there is great reward* (Ps. 19:7-11 KJV).

2. Read the verse again and list the six different ways God has spoken to man.

3. List the six benefits described in this passage.

4. *"More to be desired are they than gold, even much fine gold; sweeter also than honey and drippings of the honeycomb"* (Ps. 19:10). What does this comparison mean to you personally? Do you feel this way about God's Word? Also read: Job 22:24; Proverbs 8:10; Psalm 119:72,103.

5. *"...in keeping them there is great reward"* (Ps. 19:11). Ponder and record what you think the great reward would be? Is there a condition? How do we begin to allow God's Word permeate and work? Here are five ways to infuse the Word into your lives:

Hear ~ Romans 10:17

∾ Attend a Bible-believing, preaching church.

∾ Listen to edifying Christian radio and television broadcasts.

∾ Participate in a group Bible study.

Read ~ 2 Timothy 4:13

- ❧ Devise a plan to read the entire Bible in one year (three chapters a day and five chapters on Sunday).
- ❧ Review forgotten materials.
- ❧ Look for new areas of study.

Study ~ 1 Timothy 4:13

- ❧ Develop a "topics for future study" in your journal.
- ❧ Set aside a specific time to "dig into the Word."
- ❧ Complete what you start before going on to next area of interest.

Memorize ~ Psalm 119:11

- ❧ To win others ~ 1 Peter 3:15,16
- ❧ For personal growth ~ Acts 20:32
- ❧ To set a standard in your life ~ Psalm 19:7,8
- ❧ To seek guidance ~ Psalm 119:10

Meditate ~ 1 Timothy 4:15

To meditate is to think, ponder and mull over a verse so you can apply the Word of God to your life.

For added insight into God's Word, read Psalm 119 over several consecutive nights. Take note of the benefits of reading it.

❧ Projects

"GOD DOES SPEAK TO US—THROUGH OUR THOUGHTS AND CIRCUMSTANCES, BUT PRIMARILY THROUGH HIS WORD."

Hannah Hunnard (*Walking Among the Unseen*)

1. Look for reading lists that meet your family's specifications. Select books and create a reading plan for your leisure time.

2. Create a "reading chronicle" of the books you have read, using our for. As the year progresses, your book list should grow! When you apply for collage admission, check to see if they will take your reading chronicle into account. See our resources for a book chronicle you can copy to record the books you have read.

3. Evaluate all your books through the filter of Philippians 4:8:

Finally, brothers, whatever is true, whatever is noble, whatever is right, whatever is pure, whatever is lovely, whatever is admirable—if anything is excellent or praise-worthy—think about such things.

4. Create and hold each other accountable for a plan of Bible memorization. Plan to work on it together. You might memorize a verse, a chapter, or even a whole book.

5. When doing a Bible study, do an in-depth study of a certain passage using the form in our resource section.

❧ *Resources*

"NO ONE IS OBLIGATED TO WASTE AN HOUR TODAY OVER A WORTHLESS OR WICKED BOOK BECAUSE THERE ARE SO MANY GOOD BOOKS TO CHOOSE FROM."

Book List

Here is a smattering of books and authors my family has delighted in reading:

All Creatures Great and Small and others by James Herriot
Animal Farm by George Orwell

Brave New World by Aldous Huxley

The Cross and the Switchblade by David Wilkerson

David Copperfield and others by Charles Dickens

Emma, Pride and Prejudice, Sense and Sensibility and others by Jane Austen

Experience the Depths of Jesus Christ by Madame Jeanne Guyon

Fairy Tale of My Life (autobiography of Hans Christian Anderson)

The Good Earth by Pearl S. Buck

Heart of Darkness by Joseph Conrad

Hind's Feet on High Places and others by Hannah Hunnard

House of Seven Gables by Nathaniel Hawthorne

Jane Eyre and others by Charlotte Bronte

Life of Columbus and others by Washington Irving

Metamorphosis by Franz Kafka

Moby Dick and others by Herman Melville

Murder on the Orient Express by Agatha Christie

Prisoner of Zenda and others by Anthony Hope Hawkins

Quo Vadis by Henryk Sienkiewicz

The Hiding Place and others by Corrie Ten Boon

The Secret to a Happy Christian Life and others by Hannah Whitall Smith

Vanity Fair by William Makepeace Thackery

Who Should We Then Read? by Jan Bloom

I just met this fellow book lover and discovered her book containing lists of great authors and books for children and young adults. To order, call 320-286-5676 or e-mail: books-bloom@yahoo.com.

Reading Chronicle

Date	Author	Book Title

❧ In-depth Study

Scripture:	Observations and Questions:	Word Definitions:

Cross References:	Notes:	Interpretations:	Application and Art:

The Higher Education

> "EDUCATION: THAT WHICH DISCLOSES TO THE WISE
> AND DISGUISES FROM THE FOOLISH THEIR LACK OF
> UNDERSTANDING."
>
> *Ambrose Rierce*

E HEAR A GREAT DEAL ABOUT MOD-ERN scholarship and higher education. Sometimes there seems to be an impression in the air that there never was any learning worth speaking of except for that of a college education. Now there cannot be a greater mistake than to suppose that facilities and appliances and extensive and extended opportunities have made us giants, whereas those who went before us were pygmies. A glance at our libraries shows us volumes filled with research. The masters of literature and art still color our thought and demand our attention. Still are there old men and gray-haired women who are well and liberally educated, though the methods of their youth were somewhat different from those which their grandchildren follow. The remembrance that, not the amount that one studies, but the

degree of integration into one's thinking and knowledge, is the important thing. Colleges largely mold and influence men and woman and strongly impress their ideology on their graduates. And yet, there may be culture to be found outside college walls.

To the person who is not able to go on with their education, let me say that all of life is an academy. On every hand there are gates ajar, awaiting only the resolute touch of a man in earnest to push them open. One determined upon being well-educated need never despair of realizing his ideal.

For one thing, books are the best possible, as well as the most friendly, teachers. You may have very little time for a book, but use the little. The five or ten minutes in the morning, the spell borrowed from your luncheon hour, read with intention and attack a real book, a genuine volume of essays or poetry or history, and at the end of three months you will be surprised at the progress you have made. (I must caution the enthusiastic student against the prodigal use of sight by poring over small print in places where the light is imperfect. One's own common sense dictates care of those useful and loyal servants, the eyes.) Books are to be had in marvelously inexpensive editions. If they are bought one by one they are a wise investment for one's own home and one's life. If they are borrowed from a library, they are equally valuable friends. The person who reads daily according to a prearranged plan, and not merely for amusement, cannot fail to become cultivated. There are, among our chief literary favorites, men who never saw the inside of college walls, but whose books are the lingering delight of thousands. We need not fear that we will be ill-educated even if our college must be the real world of work.

Companionship with well-mannered and thoughtful men and women is stimulating and educational. It lifts us from the dreary level of the commonplace and rouses our finer ambitions. Perhaps we have gradually suffered ourselves to fall in a rut. It may be that we have unknowingly adopted the attitude that money is the most desirable thing in the world or that a great fortune is to be envied and the toil exerted to attain it seen as a worthy means to an end. Too many of us are like the author Bunyan's man, a character with the muck-rake who could not lift his eyes from the ground, and who was forever drawing up sticks and straws and rubbish with his poor rake. The time spent with bright, breezy, well-informed people, whose outlook is beyond the mere confines of today, who talk about large concerns and care what happens outside their immediate front doors, is blessed education for those who are admitted to it.

Travel is one of the most broadening influences which ever touches human experience. It is not in everyone's power to enjoy this, for some have not that free foot which can roam where it will. Others lack the funds, and others are bound by home duties. Here again books step in to aid us, and we may be accomplished pilgrims, even if we never stray from beyond the fireside. With heroic missionaries and valiant explorers for our guides, we may penetrate unknown regions, eat strange fares and learn the ways of odd and mysterious people. The next best thing to going to another land in person is being conducted yonder by one who has seen and noted what he saw and written it down for our learning.

I cannot too highly recommend to the young friend who seeks the best culture to establish a pattern of steady and persistent churchgoing. Not here and there to listen to gifted divines and splendid preachers, but to one's own sanctuary, to sit under one's own pastor, week in and week out. The pulpit deals with elevated themes and the minister's office is to instruct. The hearer who goes to church should go not to be critical, not to find fault, not to be inattentive, but to give well-mannered attention, and to maintain a receptive attitude of mind while in the pew. He will be unknowingly absorbing a sort of culture which is one of the best gifts the Church bestows upon her worshiping throngs. One does not go to church primarily for intellectual enrichment, but this follows in the wake of other and more spiritual privileges.

By all means, get the best education you can. Get the fullest, the highest and the widest. Go to college, if that is possible. Do not make the blunder of underrating the smaller college. It may do, as it oftentimes does, more for the girl than the larger university can. It is what you carry to the college quite as much as what the college conveys to you which makes the gracious womanhood. But if college doors are closed in your face, go bravely and confidently forward. You may still obtain the highest education if you are serious, have pluck and perseverance and a belief in yourself and in God. There is culture where there is not college and more depends on the student than on the professors. For some fine souls the world proves the best alma mater.

❧ *Mother to Mother*

"AND WE KNOW THAT ALL THINGS WORK TOGETHER FOR
GOOD TO THOSE WHO LOVE GOD, TO THOSE WHO ARE
CALLED ACCORDING TO HIS PURPOSE."

Romans 8:28

Two married years and two children later, I came to the momentous conclusion that the noble profession of nursing was not "family friendly." My wise mother counseled me to get some more education and join the professional rank of teacher. The benefits were great! No nights, weekends, holidays or on-call hours. After careful research and much thought, I presented my well-laid plan to my husband. I would attend the local college for three more years and get my teaching degree. By the time my children were in school, I would be finished. The children could be with me—sort of—at the daycare provided by the college. A significant amount of the credits I had already earned could be used toward this degree. Simple! Perfect! Wrong! My husband gave me a very clear answer. "No." He wanted me to be with the children as much as possible and continue to work nights, weekends, holidays and be on call. I was devastated.

Later that night, I crept out of bed to have a conference with God about my husband. "Lord!" I cried out, "this was the perfect plan! I love teaching my children so I know I would be a great teacher! Why are you doing this? Why is Bob being so stubborn?" A still small voice answered me, saying, "What you want and what I want are two different things." I later found out this was a paraphrase of Isaiah 55:8-9. This quiet, but convincing statement was my answer. I knew God was speaking to me and that He had a better plan for my life.

Five years later, God revealed the fulfillment of this dream He had placed in my heart. Through various circumstances it became clear to my husband and me that I was to have the privilege of teaching my children at home. How could have I known that God would create in me the heart I needed to be their teacher? My dream became a reality in a way I would never have imagined.

Ladies, what are your dreams? What is God whispering to you? I pray that in this section God will guide you and your daughter to dream the dreams He has for you!

❧ *Mother's Questions*

"ONE DETERMINED UPON BEING WELL EDUCATED NEED
NEVER DESPAIR OF REALIZING HIS IDEAL."

Perhaps you have had the opportunity to go to college or be apprenticed for your higher education, or maybe life has been your academy. In either case, your attitude toward learning and education are likely to influence your daughter's view.

1. Examine your and your husband's views on education. Write down ways your views have changed since you were a young woman of fifteen.

2. The author described life as an academy. In your journal, record some of the classes life has enrolled you in. Retell some of the lessons and teachers you may have had. Analyze whether the subjects you learned could have been taught at college?

3. Think about and list what you know of your daughter's goals for higher education.

4. John Bunyon's muck-raker character from *Pilgrim's Progress* is touched on in this chapter. In your journal, define a muck-raker in your own words and/or a situation that describes this harmful characteristic. Are you a muck-raker?

5. Culture is something that needs to be continually developed. Charlotte Mason referred to the act of reading good books and continuing to develop in various areas as "Mother Culture." What are areas of culture you could develop without going to college?

6. With your husband, explore ways you could guide and encourage your daughter in areas of higher education. This could entail either going to college or continuing the process of growth when she is done with her formal studies.

✤ *Daughter's Questions*

"'FOR SOME FINE SOULS THE WORLD PROVES THE BEST
ALMA MATER.'"

1. Reflect on the above quote. Why and how might it be true? Do you know of such a "fine soul" whose alma mater is the world? Describe that individual's accomplishments in detail and why you admire him or her.

2. What are your parents' views on higher education? What are yours? How are they different? How are they the same?

3. What are your goals for your future? Prayerfully consider and record them in your journal.

4. Think about the type of education required to fulfill your life's goals? What avenues will guide you to your destination?

5. "There is culture where there is not college, and more depends on the student than on the professors." In your journal, explain why you think this statement could be true.

6. According to the author, many of us are like the muckraking character in Bunyan's *Pilgrim's Progress*. This miserable person was incapable of lifting his eyes from the ground, forever drawing up sticks, straw and rubbish with his rake. Are you like this character? How? How could you change the way you think?

✤ *Bible Study*

"DO NOT BE CONFORMED TO THIS WORLD BUT BE TRANS-
FORMED BY THE RENEWAL OF YOUR MIND, THAT YOU MAY
PROVE WHAT IS THE WILL OF GOD, WHAT IS GOOD, ACCEPT-
ABLE AND PERFECT."

Romans 12:2 KJV

Do you know with certainty that God has plan for your life? And that you can know His will concerning you?

1. Examine these promises for your life. Record them in your Bible study journal: Jeremiah 29:11; Psalm 32 :8; Proverbs 3:5,6 (record the three steps you must take to receive guidance); James 1:5; Romans 12:1,2 (record the three steps you must take to know His will and the result of following the steps prescribed).

2. Photocopy and fill out the Godly Goals page in your resource section. As you are considering your goals, read the eight ways God reveals His will in our lives. Look up each reference verse and read it. **God's will is revealed by:**

His Word ~ Psalm 119:105

No matter what situation you are in, God's Word probably has something to say about it. Look up the topic in your concordance and discover what the Bible teaches about specific subjects.

Prayer ~ Matthew 6:5-7

One of the greatest privileges is to be able to talk to God and ask for His guidance.

Precepts ~ Psalm 119

Psalm 119 repeats the word *precept* twenty-one times in the NIV. By becoming familiar with God's Word you shall be guided by the precepts and principles you learn. Also see Psalm 19:7-9.

Holy Spirit ~ Romans 8:14

This passage illustrates how the Holy Spirit will guide us even in situations that bewilder and confuse us. When you memorize verses, the Holy Spirit will remind you of them at just the right time. But you must be walking close to Him in order to hear Him.

Closed Doors ~ Acts 16:6-10

At times there will be many options or "doors" open to you. Pray that God will close the door if is not His will for your life. Expect that He will do this. Then, when the door is closed, know that God often opens a window as He did for Paul.

Circumstances ~ Genesis 37:5-10; Acts 16:6-10; Romans 8:28

Another way God guides us is through everyday circumstances in which we are placed. Your school and your family are special training grounds the Lord has chosen for you. He doesn't waste a single situation.

Supernatural Occurrences ~ Acts 12:6-10

Burning bushes, earthquakes, whirlwinds and dreams are even used by God. However, if you consider the length of the Bible, they are comparatively rare. Do not wait only for supernatural signs to confirm God's will for your life.

Wise Counsel ~ Proverbs 12:15, 13:10, 19:21

A wise counselor is one who has had experience in the area you are seeking advise. Caution! Remember, God's will for you will never, I repeat, NEVER, be contrary to the principles and examples found in the Word of God. If it is not in line with what He has said in the Bible, it is not from God.

3. Memory verse ~ Jeremiah 29:11

❧ *Projects*

"COMPANIONSHIP WITH WELL-BRED AND THOUGHTFUL MEN
AND WOMEN IS STIMULATING AND EDUCATIONAL AND UPLIFTS
US FROM THE DREARY LEVEL OF THE COMMONPLACE."

1. Set up an appointed time to meet (Mother, Father and Daughter) and discuss the different opportunities educationally that are available for you after you are done with your high-school studies. Will it be apprenticeship? College? Marriage? Assisting at home? Working in your family business?

2. How do you think God is using the gifting and the dreams your daughter may have in order to fulfill His perfect plan for her? Pray as mother and daughter together on a regular basis that God would make it clear to you what His desires for your future education are. Write down and record what He reveals to you in your journal or in your prayer journal.

3. If you are not interested in college, look for and interview people who have accomplished their goals without college. Before you begin your interview, prepare by writing down the questions you may have. Discover what path they took to arrive where they are now. Especially talk to godly people who have achieved the goals that you believe you want to achieve.

4. At your family dinner times, create a list of topics or headlines from newspapers, magazines and news journals. Be certain that the topics are uplifting and cause a person to be thoughtful. Try to compare what is occurring in your discussions to what the Bible says about this particular topic.

5. Go to your local college or surf the Internet to research possible college expenses and scholarships for your particular

field of interest. Create a file to save and organize your findings. Compare your options.

6. Begin going to Sunday morning services at church with the attitude that you are going to come away with a great treasure that can be applied to your life. Start to store up the treasures by keeping sermon notes, reviewing them during the week.

✤ *Resources*

Guide to College Majors and Career Choices

If you are contemplating higher education, this reference could be of great benefit to you. It offers clear guidelines for choosing your career, evaluating schools, ways to choose your college major, surviving the college admissions process, how to remain on a schedule when applying for college and how to find the job you want while you are going to school. This book can be found at Christian Financial Ministry: 1-800-722-1976 or www.crown.org.

Youth Exploration Survey!

For ages 13-16. Includes: *YES! Guidebook, YES! Passport, YES! Parents' Guide.* The *Career Direct™ - Youth Exploration Survey* covers four areas: personality, vocational interests, abilities and priorities. Students are aided in applying their survey results to their current activities and relationships. This survey points them toward an exciting future career. YES! is fun, informative, interactive and biblically based. YES! can be administered to individuals or groups such as Christian schools or youth groups. This book can be found at Christian Financial Ministry (see above).

Reading List for College Bound Students by Doug Estell, Michele L. Satchwell, Patricia Wright

This book contains a list of the 100 most often recommended books from top colleges around the country. It contains annotated book lists plus ideas for a high-school reading program. Available at www.bereahigh.org/100recommended.html.

Homeschoolers College Admissions Handbook: Preparing Your 13- to 18-Year-Old for a Smooth Transition by Cafi Cohen

Cafi Cohen offers invaluable information to the homeschooling parent readying his or her child for higher education, including record-keeping and organization of transcripts, details about the admissions process and financial aid and special requirements colleges request of home-schoolers. To order, e-mail: cfcohen@pacebell.net.

The Teenage Liberation Handbook: How to Quit School and Get a Real Life and Education by Grace Lewellyn

This book tells teens how to take control of their lives and get a "real life." This book encourages young people to rediscover their natural ability to educate themselves by designing a personalized education program. Available at www.amazon.com.

Godly Goals

"I DON'T KNOW WHAT YOUR DESTINY WILL BE, BUT ONE
THING I DO KNOW: THE ONLY ONES AMONG YOU WHO WILL
BE REALLY HAPPY ARE THOSE WHO HAVE SOUGHT AND
FOUND HOW TO SERVE."

Albert Schweitzer (1875–1965)

Your name and its meaning:_____
_____
_____
_____
_____

Your Life Vision

One-year vision: _____
_____
_____
_____
_____
_____
_____
_____
_____
_____
_____
_____

Five-year vision: _____

_____

_____

_____

_____

_____

_____

_____

_____

_____

_____

_____

_____

_____

Ten-year vision: _____

_____

_____

_____

_____

_____

_____

_____

_____

_____

_____

_____

_____

_____

Areas of your life:	Relation-ship with Christ	The Word	Prayer	Higher Education
Goal:				
Scripture:				
Weak Area:				
Plan or Project:				

Her Occupation

Seven

"ANY WORK IS NOBLE IF GOD CALLS YOU TO IT AND IN
IT ONE DOES HER BEST."

EW DECISIONS ARE SO IMPORTANT OR HAVE SO
many consequences depending on their issue as
the choice of an occupation. In the days of our
grandmothers, girls did not trouble their minds
very much about their future callings. Boys were,
of course, expected to go into a trade, a business
or a profession, and were trained accordingly.
Their sisters were supposed to be growing up simply for domestic life. There was no need for them to think about a career. A
little music, a little French, a little botany were all that were
needed to train a girl several generations ago. Parents took it for
granted that, while their daughters would marry and leave them,
their sons would go out into the world and become bread win-
ners, wage earners and men of affairs. Today, an occupation
beckons both sexes. Sensible young women are as eager as their
brothers to enter some active form of service. This is the period
of specialization. While the institutes of higher education give a

good deal of culture, still the young lady who wishes to succeed must choose some particular course and become proficient in it. A young woman may also be able to enroll in an apprenticeship, which certain vocations need. But the professions specialize in different areas. For example, in law or in medicine there are different branches. When we want advice we seek a specialist and pay him for the help he gives us. This help we could not obtain from the all-around practitioner who, in devoting himself to every branch, had not thoroughly mastered its minute details.

I was a visitor the other afternoon to two studios. One belongs to a man famous for his portraits of men and women. On his walls and easels are pictures so life-like that they all but speak to you. The man is not young, and the consecration of many years has given his brush its magic, made his flesh tints so fine, showed him how to catch the subtle expression of lip and chin and eye, to pose his sitters to advantage, and paint the bust and noblest phase of every character. "Did you decide to be a painter in your boyhood?" I asked. "It was not so much I that chose painting, as painting that chose me," was the answer. "I felt a call from God to take up this line, and I followed on and obeyed, though the traditions of my family were opposed to it, and I sacrificed business prospects to sit down before my easel."

I left this room and went to another where a woman, gracious and charming, spends her days in the lovely art of flower painting. She paints only flowers, and her violets, carnations, roses, her pansies, clover blooms and orchids, look so natural they might deceive the bees. To sit down before her violets made me feel the woods of spring about me on a winter's day with sweet, shy fragrance wafting itself on every zephyr. "How did you come to paint violets, dear lady?" I asked. There was a sudden lighting up of the quiet face; she smiled wistfully. "I had to," she said gently. "The violets caught me and held me fast in their net. I can do nothing else, but I can show people violets when they are too busy to seek them in their haunts."

I met a man last week to whom golden doors of opportunity had swung open from his birth. He might have been a man of science, a lawyer, a surgeon, anything he chose, but his preference was to follow on in the path where his forefathers had achieved wealth and be an honest shipping merchant. So he had begun on the ladder's lowest rung and was toiling slowly up, as anyone else in the great house might do. "I chose this occupation because it was the one for which I felt I had the most fitness," he said. "I shall never be brilliant; but I can plod steadily on the beaten track and do my day's work with any other."

To an eminent professional man, a man who has arrived at distinction and whose name is everywhere mentioned with honor and held in high esteem, I said, "How did you happen to become a doctor?" "I did not happen," he replied. "I might have been successful in some other area. Attention, plucks, singleness of aim, hard, downright work, tend to success. I might have been a teacher, for I have a knack for instructing. I know I could have been a successful travel agent, who could convince reluctant buyers that they must purchase my wares, but I saw that my town needed a good doctor and I gave my whole mind to that. I always liked to nurse ailing chickens and dogs when I was a boy, and I have never regretted my choice. My goal was to be the best doctor in the State before I am done."

Avoid, dear young lady, the foolish fallacy that one kind of work is more noble and dignified than another. Any work is noble if God calls you to it and in it one does her best. Let your training be thorough. Then, when the time comes for your choice, choose wisely. Take parents, teachers, pastor and friends into your counsel and weigh the pros and cons. Once having chosen, stick to your choice. Chauncey Depew, addressing a graduating class in college, said, "Young men, I give you three magical words: stick, dig, save."

In entering your life's work, I cannot improve on these words. But I add a fourth word: pray. And this is perhaps the most practical word of the four. The act of prayer, if it is one of faith, brings the pledged assistance of Heaven to us in our hour of need. The wisdom of God, the tenderness, the instant help are promised to us when your Lord says, *"Ask, and it will be given to you; seek, and you will find..."* (Matt. 7:7). There is a beautiful old story of the prophet and his servant at the gate of Samaria, the prophet serene, the servant afraid. *"Lord, open his eyes that he may see!"* cried the man of God. *"And lo! The mountain was radiant with an angel host, the chariots and horses sent from the skies for the help of Elisha"* (2 Kings 6:17).

❧ *Mother to Mother*

"A MAN'S HEART PLANS HIS WAY, BUT THE LORD DIRECTS HIS
STEPS."

Proverbs 16:9

"What? You mean you don't have a room for me?" I could hear the plaintive and slightly irritated voice of Laura, my daughter, on the phone. It was only three weeks before classes began at the Christian college and she had begun to wonder why she hadn't heard of the selection of her roommate. Her curiosity had gotten the better of her and she called the admission office. It was during that call she got the news.

She had planned to attend a Christian university in our state. She would stay in their dorms and take a minimum number of classes while taking the bulk of her classes at the state university that specialized in her area of interest. This involved a great amount of effort and planning. She had gone to the campus several times over the previous two years and talked to counselors and advisors. Laura even attended classes and stayed at the dorm to get the feel of the place. We all just knew this was God's plan. So you can imagine our confusion when a minor technicality left our daughter without a place to stay in a strange town.

We thought we had her first year all planned out. We prayed, investigated and pursued every avenue to make sure this was His will. When this happened, my daughter asked, "Why would God not want me in a Christian college?" I didn't know the answer. All I knew was that God was in control; He could see the unseen. I offered her Jeremiah 29:11: *"For I know the plans I have for you, declares the Lord, plans to prosper you and not to harm you, plans to give you hope and a future."* What an opportunity to teach and model trust. Within the week, the Lord moved in a miraculous way to ensure His plan for our daughter. He provided an apartment in walking distance, two roommates that our family loves, Christian friends and all at a secular university. How gratifying to hear from her now: "Mom, I can now see that His hand was at work and that God had a better plan for me."

When plans change, how should we respond? Often we agonize and brood because we don't have the control we would like to have. It is in these moment we need to step back, trust God, and wait to see how He will use the situation for His glory.

❧ *Mother's Questions*

"LIFE IS A PROMISE; FULFILL IT."

Mother Teresa (1910–1997)

1. What does this quote by Mother Teresa mean to you? Do you believe your life is a promise? Have you or are you in the process of fulfilling it? In your journal, elaborate on what you think your promise is and give an explanation of your thoughts.

2. Margaret Sangster wrote, in this last chapter, of four ways men and women chose their professions. Reread the chapter and list the ways in your journal.

3. If you were to choose one thing that compelled you to choose your occupation, what would it be? Is it one of the reasons discussed in this chapter? Do you know what compelled your husband to choose his occupation? If not, ask him and record your findings in your journal.

4. In your opinion, what is the noblest form of work and why? Do you think certain occupations are more noble than others? How do you view your role as mother?

5. There are four words that Margaret gives as advice for the reader. Recall what they are and what they mean to you.

6. As mothers, we have many hopes, dreams and goals for our daughters. In your journal, write a prayer from your heart for your daughter's future.

❧ Daughter's Questions

"THE PERSON BORN WITH A TALENT THEY ARE MEANT TO USE WILL FIND THEIR GREATEST HAPPINESS IN USING IT."

Johann Wolfgang Von Goethe (1749–1832)

1. Read the quote from Von Goethe again. Do you believe this is a true or false statement? Give reasons to support your answers. Do you have a clear vision of the talent you were born

to use? If so write about your talent and how it could be used. If not ask your mother or others who know you well what they see as a talent.

2. Read Chapter Seven again and discover the four different reasons men and women chose their professions. List the four reasons in your journal.

3. In reading over the four reasons that compelled the subjects to choose their occupations which one reason seems most like one you would choose?

4. Do you feel one form of work is more noble than another? If you could think of one job that might be elevated above others, what would it be? What makes you believe it is admirable? What qualities must an occupation have to be noble?

5. In this chapter, the author gives four directions for true success. List them and discuss what they mean to you. How could you apply this advice to your life?

6. Undoubtedly you have many dreams, goals and hopes for what your future might be. Write out a prayer from your heart to the Lord about your desires for the future.

✬ *Bible Study*

"BUT EVERY MAN HATH HIS PROPER GIFT OF GOD, ONE AFTER THIS MANNER, AND ANOTHER AFTER THAT."

1 Corinthians 7:7

God has given us very clear instructions and teaching in His Word about spiritual gifts. In this Bible study, you will discover what some of the gifts are, who they are given by and why and how we are to use them.

1. Read 1 Corinthians 12:1-30.

2. Read verses 4-6 over again and record in your journal all the facts you learn about the various gifts.

3. For what reason is the manifestation of the Spirit given?

4. In your journal, list the various gifts discussed in vv. 8-10.

5. By whom are all the gifts given? Do you see any evidence in these Scriptures that we can decide on what gifts we want?

6. Read vv. 12-26. To what are the individual believers compared to? Could you use this analogy in your family? Can you see the various gifts and roles that your brothers and sisters play in your family? Can you see the various gifts and roles that your brothers and sisters in the Lord play in your spiritual family? In your journal write down your observations.

7. From what you have read, can there be unity and harmony amidst the diversity of the spiritual gifts of the saints?

8. In your journal, document all the gifts you find. In a concordance or topical Bible, look up references for each gift. Read and make a list of the verses you find. This exercise will give you a clearer picture of the various gifts and how they are used.

9. Memory Verse ~ 1 Corinthians 7:7

10. Extra Reading ~ 1 Corinthians 13 -14; Ephesians 4:7; Matthew 2:14-30; Romans 12:6-8.

❧ *Projects*

"OUR DEEDS DETERMINE US, AS MUCH AS WE DETERMINE OUR DEEDS."

George Elliot (1819–1880)

1. Together, sit down and make a list of the various spiritual gifts that a person may exhibit. Mother, this would be a

good time to discuss the gifting you see in your daughter and ask her to name the spiritual gifts she believes she possesses.

2. Encourage your daughter to take a career planning test such as *Finding the Career that Fits You,* available from www.crown.org or from Christian Financial Counseling.

3. Corinthians 12:1 states, *"Now about the spiritual gifts, brothers, I do not want you to be ignorant."* With your daughter, take one of the spiritual gift tests named in the resource section of this chapter.

4. Brainstorm and develop a plan to utilize daughter's gifting. For example, if she has the gift of compassion and wants to work in the health field, she could volunteer in a nursing home. She might plan family holiday menus and events or invite other families as guests if she wants to develop a gift of hospitality.

5. Plan to read various books together on the subject of spiritual gifts and aptitudes. Educate yourself as much as possible so you can assist your daughter in her career planning.

6. Commit to pray together about your daughter's future. Ask God to clarify her gifts. Ask Him to open the doors He wants open and to bar any way she should not go.

❧ *Resources*

"NOW ABOUT SPIRITUAL GIFTS, BROTHERS, I DO NOT WANT YOU TO BE IGNORANT."

1 Corinthians 12:1

All items in this section can be found at Crown Financial Ministries, P.O. Box 100, Gainesville, GA 30503-0100.

Personality Plus for Parents: Understanding What Makes Your Child Tick by Florence Littauer

All kids are not the same, and neither are parents. How can all of you get along? Dynamic speaker and best-selling author Florence Littauer uses proven principles from her popular *Personality Plus* to show parents how to raise their children individually and take cues from each child's temperament and personality.

The Path Finder by Lee Ellis

This is another resource book designed for people making career decisions. It focuses on practical steps for evaluating career decisions and occupations, teaches you how search for a job, write a resume and perform in an interview, all while offering sound Biblical perspective.

Finding the Career That Fits You by Lee Ellis and Larry Burkett

Suitable for individual or group use, this workbook includes a personality analysis as well as surveys for examining your interest, skills and work priorities. Through this self-assessment process, you will gain a clear understanding of your pattern for work.

Money Management for College Students by Larry Burkett

Preparing for college can be overwhelming. What career should you pursue? Which college should you attend? How will you pay for your education? This book answers those questions and more!

Notes

Notes

Notes

Notes

Order Form

To order additional copies of *Winsome Womanhood ~Day-break~* please use the order form below (please print):

Name: _____

Address: _____

City: _____ State/Prov: _____

Zip/Postal Code: _____ Telephone: _____

_____copies @ $13.95 US / $18.95 Cdn.: $_____

Shipping: ($3.00 first book – $1.00 each add. book) $_____

Texas residents add 8.25% Sales Tax: $_____

Total amount enclosed: **$**_____

Payable by Check, Money Order, VISA or MasterCard
(indicate which credit card)

Credit Card #:_____ Exp. Date:_____

Signature:_____

Send to: *Pumpkin Seed Press*
43668 355th Ave.
Humphrey, Nebraska
68642 USA
(or call Toll Free) 877-923-1682